WE JUST NEED A FEW MORE SMART PEOPLE TO HELP US GET THERE ...

MACHINE LEARNING
GRAPH ALGORITHMS
DATA MINING CLUSTERS
AUTONOMOUS SYSTEMS
CLUSTER AUTOMATIONS
COLLABORATIVE FILTERING
NATURAL LANGUAGE PROCESSING
DISTRIBUTED SYSTEMS
TEXT CATEGORIZATION
CLUSTERING

YAHOO! SEARCH®

careers.yahoo.com

Make:
technology on your time™

Volume 01

22

The feral robot dogs are coming to a Superfund site near you.

The Wright brothers made better bicycle seats than airplanes. It's time to revisit the grooved saddle.

38

ON THE COVER
Photographer Emily Nathan captures Cris Benton rigging his kite camera before a test run. Make one yourself with his instructions on page 50. The kite shown is a Cody historical reproduction, made by Logo Kites Drachen GmbH of Hamburg, Germany. Available exclusively from Gomberg Kite Productions International, *www.gombergkites.com.*

ABOVE ALL BE ORIGINAL

It's often the smallest details that make the biggest difference and create products that stand out from the crowd. Take for example the tiny sensor that sits on top of our BeoVision 5. Its magic 'eye' registers the changing light conditions in the room and automatically adjusts the picture's color, contrast and brightness to match. This enables you to enjoy the perfect viewing experience – even in broad daylight. See it for yourself at your nearest Bang & Olufsen store or call us for a complimentary home consultation. BeoVision 5: 42" plasma, active loudspeaker system, multiple placement options.

www.bang-olufsen.com

Make: Projects

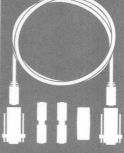

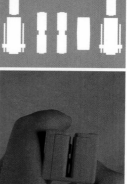

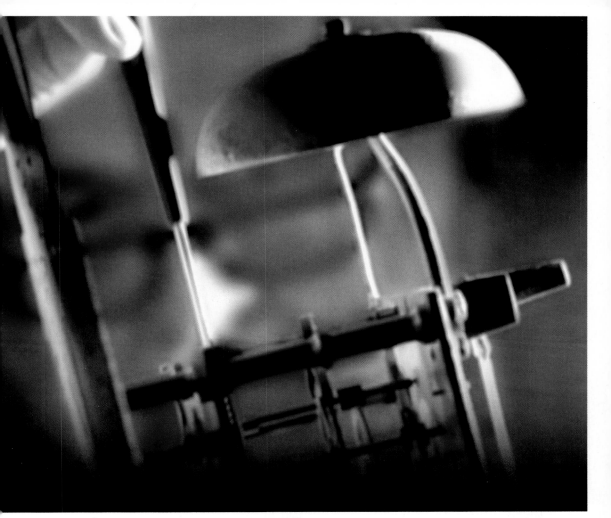

Precision Craftsmanship Requires Precision Tools.

Kronus, the premium tool line only at RadioShack.

Take pride in your work? Then you owe it to yourself to discover Kronus™ tools, now at RadioShack. Kronus tools are precision-crafted out of the finest materials and ergonomically engineered to deliver the highest degree of performance and comfort.

In fact, we're so confident of Kronus tools' quality, we put it in writing— because Kronus tools come with a limited lifetime warranty.* Complement your dedication to quality and craftsmanship with tools that meet your exacting standards – Kronus tools, only at RadioShack.

Volume 01

Even if you've never picked up a soldering iron, MAKE's primer will have you connecting components in short order.

Why is this man screaming? Because his mechanical pong machine has broken yet again.

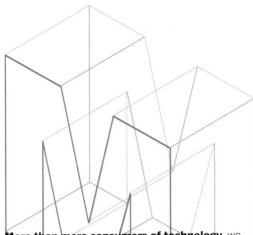

Dale Dougherty

The Making of Make:

More than mere consumers of technology, we are *makers*, adapting technology to our needs and integrating it into our lives. Some of us are born *makers* and others, like me, become *makers* almost without realizing it.

Maybe it started when I burned my first music CD, ripping individual songs from packaged CDs and assembling my own playlist. This was unthinkable just five years ago, and now it's how we make our own music — much to the chagrin of the recording music industry.

Maybe it started when I got Wi-Fi working, not just for myself but for my whole family. Suddenly, the computer wasn't locked down to a desk and wired to an outlet. It was free to roam, like a cellphone, and I began finding new places such as coffee houses that I could call home, or at least home-office.

Maybe it started when I brought my digital camera and laptop on vacation and found that my slideshow was ready before the vacation was even over.

I'm sure that most of us share these experiences, and many others that demonstrate the impact of new technologies in our lives. Think of how many devices each of us interacts with on a regular basis today. And that's only the beginning. Neil Gershenfeld of MIT's Center for Bits and Atoms, who is featured in this issue, writes in his book *When Things Start to Think* that "personal computing has not gone far enough; it lets us shape our digital environment but not our physical environment." In other words, technology that allows us to create complex things will soon become as affordable as the technology we use to create and manage data. We are just beginning to see the impact of technology in our personal lives. So much is possible.

MAKE is a new magazine dedicated to showing how to make technology work for you. At the core of the magazine are projects that show you how to use technology in interesting and practical ways. A MAKE project is rewarding and fun as an experience, and it produces something you can share with your friends and family. Becoming a *maker* is a lot like learning how to become a better cook — you can follow or improvise upon the work of experts.

In the process of developing MAKE, I have met all kinds of expert *makers* who were excited to contribute their ideas and their favorite projects. There are some I'd call *extreme makers* who bring highly specialized skills and experience working with both new and old technology. They specialize in the unexpected and go beyond what you or I would ever consider practical. We can learn a lot by following what they do, and I'm happy that MAKE provides a showcase for their work.

I hope you enjoy getting to know the experts as well as meeting other *makers* like yourself. We expect that our website will become a place to share your experiences building the projects in the magazine, as well as a home for projects that you develop. I look forward to meeting you there.

Let me know what you think of MAKE and how you use technology to make your own life better. You can contact me at dale@oreilly.com.

Dale Dougherty is the editor and publisher of MAKE and the publisher of O'Reilly Network (*www.oreillynet.com*).

It's ironic that in an industry

so concerned with memory,

how quickly we forget.

Luckily we have a place to remind us. The Computer History Museum is dedicated to exploring the computing revolution and its impact on the human experience. It is home to the largest collection of computing-related artifacts in the entire world. The collection includes hardware, software, photos, films and video, documents and many one-of-a-kind and rare objects. The Museum's many programs include a popular speaker series featuring luminaries and their personal stories, commemorative celebrations and oral histories that are sure to jog your memory. The Computer History Museum. *Where Computing History Lives*

COMPUTER HISTORY MUSEUM

1401 N Shoreline Blvd Mountain View CA 94043
tel 650 810 1010

www.computerhistory.org

Make:
technology on your time™

EDITOR AND PUBLISHER
Dale Dougherty
dale@oreilly.com

EDITOR IN CHIEF
Mark Frauenfelder
mark@boingboing.net

CREATIVE DIRECTOR
David Albertson
david@albertsondesign.com

MANAGING EDITOR
Shawn Connally

ART DIRECTOR
Kirk von Rohr

ASSOCIATE EDITOR
Phillip Torrone

DESIGN INTERN
Dennis Pasco

EDITORIAL ASSISTANT
Arwen O'Reilly

ASSOCIATE PUBLISHER, MARKETING
Dan Woods

COPY CHIEF
Mary Hubben

COPY EDITORS/RESEARCH
**Goli Mohammadi,
Michael Shapiro**

ADVERTISING DIRECTOR
Colette McMullen
707-827-7175
colette@oreilly.com

WEBMASTER
Terrie Miller

PUBLISHER AT LARGE
John Battelle

WEB DESIGN
Laura Schmier

PUBLISHED BY O'REILLY MEDIA, INC.
**Tim O'Reilly, CEO
Laura Baldwin, COO**

MAKE TECHNICAL ADVISORY BOARD:
**Gareth Branwyn, Joe Grand,
Saul Griffith, Natalie Jeremijenko**

Volume 01, February 2005
MAKE ™ is published quarterly by O'Reilly Media, Inc., in the months of February, May, August, and November. O'Reilly Media is located at 1005 Gravenstein Hwy North, Sebastopol, CA 95472, 707-827-7000. SUBSCRIPTIONS: Send all subscription requests to: MAKE, P.O. Box 17046, North Hollywood, CA 91615-7046 or subscribe online at *makezine.com/offer* or via phone at 866-289-8847 (U.S. and Canada), all other countries call 818-487-2037. Subscriptions are available for $34.95 for 1 year (4 quarterly issues) in the U.S. Canada: $39.95 USD; all other countries: $49.95 USD.

Please note: Technology, the laws, and limitations imposed by manufacturers and content owners, are constantly changing. Thus, some of the projects described may not work, may be inconsistent with current laws or user agreements, or may damage or adversely affect some equipment.

Your safety is your own responsibility, including proper use of equipment and safety gear, and determining whether you have adequate skill and experience. Power tools, electricity and other resources used for these projects are dangerous, unless used properly and with adequate precautions, including safety gear. Some illustrative photos do not depict safety precautions or equipment, in order to show the project steps more clearly. These projects are not intended for use by children.

Use of the instructions and suggestions in MAKE is at your own risk. O'Reilly Media, Inc., disclaims all responsibility for any resulting damage, injury, or expense. It is your responsibility to make sure that your activities comply with applicable laws, including copyright.

NEW LEAF PAPER
ENVIRONMENTAL BENEFITS STATEMENT

This magazine is printed on New Leaf Legacy, made with 10% post-consumer waste, elemental chlorine free. By using this environmentally friendly paper, Make Magazine saved the following resources:

trees	water	energy	solid waste	greenhouse gases
77 fully grown	30,233 gallons	41 million BTUs	3,594 pounds	6,955 pounds

Calculated based on research done by Environmental Defense and other members of the Paper Task Force.

© New Leaf Paper Visit us in cyberspace at www.newleafpaper.com or call 1-888-989-5323

Contributors

Joe Grand ("Soldering & Desoldering") describes himself as "anal, goofy, high-strung, and obsessed with work." He grew up in Boston and has been involved in electronics since he was 7 years old. "Hardware hacking is, to me, a perfect example of 'anti-establishment'. Make a product do something it was never intended to do, add a personal touch, and make it your own. Not just buying a product and using it as is (which is what The Man wants you to do!)." Besides working on secret projects involving video games, toys, and consumer electronics for his company, Grand Idea Studio, Inc., Joe lives in San Diego where he runs, swims, cycles, and plays the drums.

Andrew "Bunnie" Huang ("Glowstick A Go-Go") simply put, is an engineer. The Cardiff by the Sea, Calif., resident says he's somewhat of a hacker because he likes to explore complex systems and understand them at a deep level. "I've always liked the smell of new electronics. I think it is like the smell of a new adventure. Every time I get a new piece of hardware, I like to look inside and learn everything I can from visual inspection."

Blaming his father for his hacker sensibilities, Bunnie says, "He would never let me touch electronic parts because they contained harmful compounds like lead. That just made me more curious about the subject." Bunnie now spends his time designing nanophotonic integrated circuits for a startup company, Luxtera. He's also a big fan of electronic music, both from a DJ and dance perspective.

Billy Hoffman ("Magnetic Stripe Reader") says he is too curious for his own good. "I like to take things apart, see how they work, see their shortcomings, and try to make them better."

Living in Atlanta gives him plenty of time to pursue outdoor activities as well as seek input from his friends about possible technological advances he's working on. Some of Billy's current projects include a self-destructing hard drive, some radio frequency ID stuff, blogging technology, and spyware-cracking software. He's graduating this spring from the Georgia Institute of Technology with a computer science degree — anyone hiring?

As an illustrator who straddles the worlds of art and science, **Nik Schulz** ("Kite Aerial Photography," "$14 Video Camera Stabilizer," and "5-in-1 Network Cable") loves to make things and has always appreciated well-drawn instructions. Working on the illustration for the Kite Aerial Photography project was inspirational to him. "I remember thinking how amazingly thorough and well-presented Charles Benton's reference work was. The rig itself was also a triumph. He had created a product that reflected truly exceptional standards of design, function, and aesthetics, out of materials as humble as rubber bands and popsicle sticks."

The San Francisco resident continued, "It reinforced the idea that good design doesn't have to be expensive and that, in fact, the best design makes the most use out of the fewest resources. To have the opportunity to help illuminate these really clever projects for others is really enjoyable for me."

Photographer **Emily Nathan** ("Welcome to the Fab Lab" and "Kite Aerial Photography") became interested in photography because her dad had an Olympus OM-10 camera and a subscription to *National Geographic*. "I became obsessed early on with the *The New York Times Magazine* and with pictures my dad had taken in vegetable markets in Israel."

Attending art camps and taking shop class while growing up gave her a fondness for scientists and makers of all kinds. She herself has taken apart her fair share of calculators. Emily lives with her husband in San Francisco in a 100-year-old Victorian apartment when she's not surfing, shooting photos, or traveling, all of which she's been known to do at relatively the same time.

Contributing Artists:
Jorge Colombo, eBoy.com, Christopher Hujanen, Timmy Kucynda, Mike Martin, Evan McNary, Emily Nathan, Dennis Pasco, Nik Schulz, Damien Scogin, Kirk von Rohr, Carlin Wing

Contributing Writers:
Tim Anderson, Charles C. Benton, Tom Bridge, Simon DeDeo, D.C. Denison, Cory Doctorow, Daniel M. East, Simon Quellen Field, Rob Flickenger, Joseph Fung, Joe Grand, Saul Griffith, Alex Handy, Kaden Harris, David and Raina Hawley, Billy Hoffman, Bunnie Huang, Mark Hurst, Mister Jalopy, Xeni Jardin, Brian Jepson, Todd Lappin, Johnny Lee, Wei-Meng Lee, William Lidwell, Geoffrey Litwack, Merlin Mann, Matthew MacDonald, Dave Mathews, Marc H. Nathan, Danny O'Brien, J.W. Olson, Tim O'Reilly, Peter Orosz, Michael Ossmann, Robin Outis, Gareth Palidwor, Bob Parks, David Pescovitz, Michael Rattner, Justin Ried, Dori Smith, Paul Spinrad, Bruce Sterling, Simon St.Laurent, Howard Wen, Steve Wood

YAK SHAVING

Stuck in the middle of a stack
of stuff you're supposed to do?
Sharpen your wool clippers.
By Danny O'Brien and Merlin Mann

Illustration by Dennis Pasco

WE AT LIFE HACKS LABS HAVE dedicated our careers to understanding how geeks hack their own lives to become super-productive monsters of speed and acuity. This has, unfortunately, led many people to assume that we are in some way super-organized ourselves.

Oh, as if. Nothing could be further from the truth. It's sort of like confusing the territory with the map, or the glamorous fashion supermodel with the creepy guys hanging out at the stage door, taking notes on everything she does.

We are those creepy guys (metaphorically, at least). We're trying to get our own lives sorted, and that's why we spend all our time staring at and standing disturbingly close to the effective geeks. It's hard work, and the longer you work at it, the harder it appears to be.

Take writing this article. Looks like a perfectly constrained job, doesn't it? Write a few words, paste them into an email, and send it to whatever home-made, clanking machine made of string, cornstarch, and organic squid ink the MAKE staff uses to construct the magazine. It turns out, however, that the time and effort expended between writing that first word and just reaching this paragraph has, by our estimates, been almost infinite.

It has required, among other duties, a careful cost-benefit analysis of whether to write it using Microsoft Word or a text editor using DocBook Lite XML; the meticulous examination of four Wikipedia articles (including re-editing two of them); the compromise coding of a plaintext-to-RTF conversion utility; several great pizzas; and a two-hour Googling distraction into exactly how one might make machines out of string and cornstarch.

About the only thing we didn't do was A) get the piece in on time, and B) shave a yak.

Well, that's only partly true. Actually, all of this was yak shaving. Yak shaving is the technical term* for when you find yourself eight levels deep — and possibly in a recursive loop — in a stack of jobs.

You start out deciding to tidy your room, and you realize in order to do that you'll need some more trash bags, so you need to go to the shops, which will involve you getting out the car, but the car needs gas, so you'll need to go to the gas station first, which means that you should probably find your gas discount card, which involves finding your keys, which are in this room somewhere...

What can we do? Our anti-yak-shaving research is still ongoing (current estimates indicate between five minutes and 50 years before we have it licked). But we've got some guesses as to why hackers hit the problem more than others.

The problem is problems. We like solving puzzles. And, if we were honest, we'd admit that some of us like solving puzzles a bit more than we like solved puzzles. And, thanks to our upbringing in the infinitely tinkerable world of computers, we subconsciously believe that any problem is a puzzle to be fixed. When you have a Swiss Army knife of a mind, everything looks like it should be dismantled.

Other people — you know, people who actually get things done — don't have this problem. Much of the world, to them, is locked up, nailed to the floor, not something they can do much about. They navigate around mountains, rather than invent a new sort of crampon.

> ## "Some of us like solving puzzles a bit more than we like solved puzzles."

Super-efficient hackers, we think, do something slightly different. They learn when to say no to the temptation of endless fiddling.

We're trying to get to that state ourselves. And, like anyone attempting to fix some busted code, the first step is sticking in a few breakpoints.

So, here's the Life Hack we're giving you: have a notepad (real or computer), and whenever you find yourself spawning a new sub-task, stop, record your task-switch, and note why you're doing it. The act of writing itself may give you pause: is this problem-solving really necessary? If it really is an essential task, you'll at least have a reminder of what you set out to achieve — and what that job was that you're supposed to be returning to.

Solving the world's problems is something good hackers achieve, often as a side effect. But you don't have to spend all your time lost in your own life's subroutines — even if that's where the best fun is to be had.

*Don't believe us? Check the Jargon File: *www.catb.org/~esr/jargon/html/Y/yak-shaving.html*

Learn how to shave your yak more efficiently at Danny O'Brien's *lifehacks.com* and Merlin Mann's *43folders.com*.

GAUSS RIFLE By Simon Quellen Field

A linear accelerator for studying high-energy physics costs around $5 billion. But you can make one for about 30 bucks with four strong magnets, a wooden ruler, some plastic tape, and nine steel balls.

This easy project demonstrates the transfer of kinetic energy from one object to another. More importantly, it also shoots a steel ball really fast at the target of your choice. When each ball strikes the magnet in front of it, its kinetic energy is transferred to the next ball down the line. By the time the fourth ball shoots off the ruler, it possesses almost four times the energy of the first ball, which means it's moving faster, too. (The speed increase is proportional to the square root of the increase in kinetic energy.) This project takes just a few minutes to build once you have the parts, which can be ordered from *scitoys.com*.

1 | GET

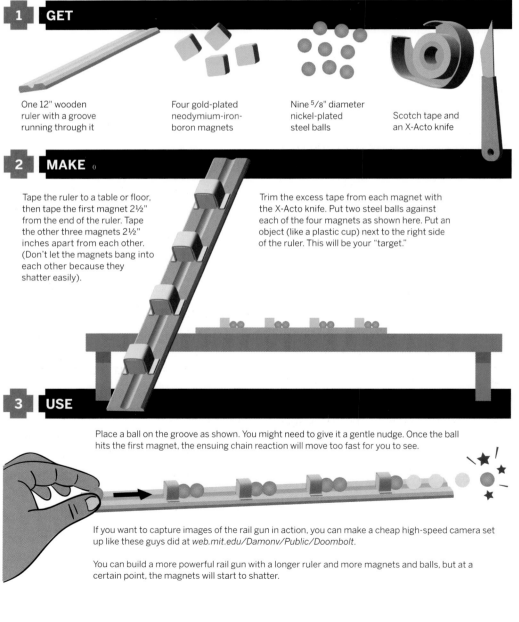

One 12" wooden ruler with a groove running through it

Four gold-plated neodymium-iron-boron magnets

Nine $5/8$" diameter nickel-plated steel balls

Scotch tape and an X-Acto knife

2 | MAKE

Tape the ruler to a table or floor, then tape the first magnet 2½" from the end of the ruler. Tape the other three magnets 2½" inches apart from each other. (Don't let the magnets bang into each other because they shatter easily).

Trim the excess tape from each magnet with the X-Acto knife. Put two steel balls against each of the four magnets as shown here. Put an object (like a plastic cup) next to the right side of the ruler. This will be your "target."

3 | USE

Place a ball on the groove as shown. You might need to give it a gentle nudge. Once the ball hits the first magnet, the ensuing chain reaction will move too fast for you to see.

If you want to capture images of the rail gun in action, you can make a cheap high-speed camera set up like these guys did at *web.mit.edu/Damonv/Public/Doombolt*.

You can build a more powerful rail gun with a longer ruler and more magnets and balls, but at a certain point, the magnets will start to shatter.

Illustrations by Mark Frauenfelder

Tim O'Reilly

NEWS FROM THE FUTURE

WILLIAM GIBSON ONCE SAID, "The future is here. It's just not evenly distributed yet." His words match up perfectly with my experience.

Time after time, I've watched people who are comfortable pushing the boundaries of technology — researchers and the kind of people who are called "hackers" in the computer world — show us something that looks like a clever trick, only to see it blossom years later into a whole new industry.

I've built my business — one of the largest and most successful computer book publishers in the world — by watching these people, whom I affection-ately call "alpha geeks," and helping the technologies they pioneer find roots in the wider world.

So, for example, when Wi-Fi was first released as a local area network (LAN) technology, we saw hackers climbing on rooftops, placing homebrewed antennas to beam their office networks down to the local coffee shop. And we knew immediately that wireless networking was going to become much more ubiquitous than its corporate backers imagined.

This column celebrates news tidbits that, to me, hint at the shape of the future. I won't draw any conclusions; I'll just share some of the news headlines that are hitting the O'Reilly Radar. Make of them what you will.

You may notice that patterns begin to emerge: ubiquitous wireless networking, ubiquitous digital image recording, the surveillance society, robots in our midst, what Freeman Dyson calls "the domesti-cation of biotechnology," automobiles and buildings as computers ripe for hacking....

Visit *makezine.com* for references to these items. In future columns, I'll drill down into some of this "news from the future."

If you are reading this magazine, you're probably one of those people who is shaping the future that's already here, so tell me what's on your radar. Send email to tim@oreilly.com.

Tim O'Reilly (*tim.oreilly.com*) is the founder and CEO of O'Reilly Media.

JAPANESE ROBOTS TO CARRY HUMANS

IMPLANTED RFID TAGS TO REPLACE CASH

INTERNET-CONTROLLED ROBOT TO BROWSE LIBRARY STACKS

MAN FLIES UNPOWERED ACROSS ENGLISH CHANNEL USING CARBON-FIBER WING STRAPPED TO HIS BACK

HOME DNA SEQUENCING KIT GOES ON SALE

WIRELESS STREET LAMPS FOR TRAFFIC MONITORING

GENETICALLY MODIFIED FLOWER DETECTS LANDMINES

ROBOT "DOG" LEARNS TO EAT "GOOD-TASTING" BLOCKS

GENE THERAPY CREATES SUPER-STRONG RATS

JAPANESE SCIENTIST INVENTS "MAGNETIC WOOD" TO BLOCK CELL PHONE SIGNALS

DIGITAL "GHOSTS" TO GUIDE STUDENTS AT COPENHAGEN UNIVERSITY

WIRELESS ACCESS POINT BUILT INTO LIGHT FIXTURE

ISRAEL DEVELOPING MICRODRONE SPY PLANES

HP EXPERIMENTS WITH "ALWAYS-ON" CAMERA

BRITISH GOVERNMENT LOBBYING FOR REMOTE CONTROL OVER AUTO ELECTRONICS TO STOP FLEEING CARS

ROBOTIC CONES CAN BE AUTOMATICALLY MOVED AROUND ON HIGHWAY

"SENSECAM" NECKLACE TAKES 2,000 IMAGES A DAY

U.S. WILL USE ROBOTS TO PATROL WATER SUPPLY

FLASH-MOB GANG WARFARE

SENSOR-ENABLED SHOE DYNAMICALLY RECONFIGURES ITSELF BASED ON CHANGING CONDITIONS

Monomania

No rational person denies that monorails are the greatest mode of urban transit ever. So **Kim Pedersen** built one in his backyard, making it the greatest backyard ever. The Niles Monorail, named for his family's Fremont, California neighborhood, treats riders to a looping, open-air journey between trees, across the back fence, above the pool, and alongside the house before making a hairpin turn over the driveway and returning to Kitchen View Station for disembarking.

The monorail's graceful track is supported by 4-inch square wooden pylons that range from five to eight feet in height, each anchored in two feet of concrete. Plain 4x8-inch beams comprise the straight sections, while curves are made from strips of ⅜-inch plywood that soaked in the pool before being bent and laminated together. The kid-size, 2-car trains run off of a 6-inch drive-wheel powered by twin motorcycle batteries and a 1-horsepower Badsey scooter motor, controlled by a 4-speed Winland WMC120 controller. One 6-hour charge,

and the monorail has enough juice to make casual runs all day long. The wood-framed cars have a painted sheet-metal exterior. A headlight in front, bellows (made of duct-tape material), and detailing inspired by Seattle's Alweg monorail complete the streamlined look.

Fifty-two-year-old Pedersen, who also founded a monorail enthusiast and advocacy group that boasts over 3,800 members in 73 countries, admits that he has a one-track mind — but now he and his kids can ride a monorail whenever they want.

—*Paul Spinrad*

≫ **The Niles Monorail:** *monorails.org/tMspages/Niles.html*

Top: The monorail took five years to make. The track runs 299 feet, 9 inches, and is supported by 36 pylons. Public transportation officials, take note: the total cost of materials for the project, including train, track, and hardware, was $4,070.07, or about $13.58 per foot. Pedersen points out that a mile-long track would run just under $72,000.

Middle: Pedersen working on the track in August 1997. After experimenting with different methods and materials to make curved sections of track, Pedersen settled on using laminated plywood, which he soaked in the family swimming pool to make it easier to shape. He says it was difficult to maintain the curved shape when he drilled the sections together.

Bottom: An early concept drawing from 1988. Pedersen started sketching plans for a backyard monorail in 1969 when he was a junior in high school. His father nixed the idea, though, so he had to wait until he had his own house to build one. He started construction on the monorail in 1996.

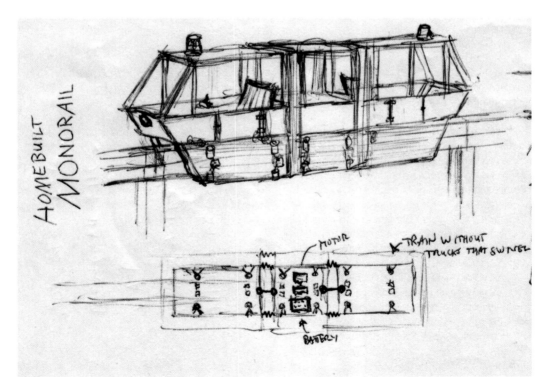

Steamed Up

If the phrase "Live Steam enthusiasts" conjures up visions of health spa devotees huddled over vapor pools, think again.

In geek parlance, it refers to the global community of model-train lovers who build quarter-scale models of steam and diesel locomotives in their home workshops using mills, lathes, and drill presses — then ride them around through large layouts in backyards or public parks. Prices for miniature, rideable locomotives can range from a few hundred dollars for one made from scavenged parts to hundreds of thousands of dollars for a high-end model with all the bells and whistles.

One popular online hub for rideable model-train fans is *livesteaming.com*, which has pointers to dozens of hobbyist clubs in Europe, Africa, Asia, and North America. The site also serves as a helpful resource for locating live-steam conventions, which take place at locations around the world and throughout the year.

In 2004, one American group organized a marathon ride in an attempt to break *The Guinness Book of Records'* standard for distance traveled in 24 hours by a rideable-scale locomotive. Using two diesel model locomotives — one powered by gasoline and the other driven by batteries — a tag team of engineers spanning three generations of railroad junkies claims to have successfully broken the 1994 record of 168 miles, set in England. One locomotive reached 218 miles, the other 208. All participants, who bypassed sleep for a day in their pursuit of greatness on the rails, achieved a satisfied state of exhaustion. —*Xeni Jardin*

≫ **Live Steaming:** *livesteaming.com*

Photograph by Trevor Heath

Desktop Wars

A few years ago, **Kaden Harris** was engraving brass nameplates for a manufacturer of "employee-recognition products" — signs, trophies, and other desktop expressions of institutional gratitude. Now his scaled-down medieval siege weapons bring heart, soul, and serious brains into the otherwise bland genre. The Vancouver-based artist handcrafts each piece out of hardwood and salvaged metal artifacts, cooks up wood stains from traditional vegetable sources, and culls antiquated hardware from swap meets and dumpsters.

Harris' post-authentic reproductions evoke a parallel universe where castle-buster gear sports brass hot-rod flames and laser sights. And because his designs follow standard formulas for optimization, they hurl their payloads (mouse balls, golf balls, bolts) impressively far — especially the ballista, which uses two tightly strung, twisted skeins that don't require heavy mass to inflict heavy damage,

unlike the counterweight-based trebuchet. Meanwhile, Harris has built prototypes for heavier-gauge artillery, including a spud gun powered by a standard butane lighter and a motorized machine that rapid-fires pencils via two counter-rotating tires, like a pitching machine. Harris' lawyer advised against selling the latter because it was just too dangerous. As Harris admits, "It's all good fun until somebody loses an eye." —*Paul Spinrad*

Left: 18-inch floating-arm trebuchet. The fulcrum is on wheels, making it much more efficient than standard trebuchets.

Right: 17-inch guillotine. The blade is weighted with a ½-pound block of lead.

≫ **Eccentric Genius:** *eccentricgenius.ca*

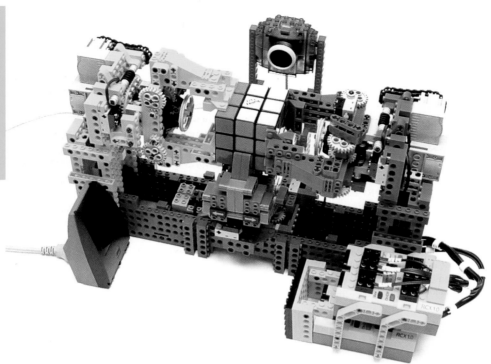

Block Head

Like an Olympian shirking drug charges, **Jonathan Brown** wants people to know that he's never been a *grinder*. A Lego builder who holds a day job as a conservator at the Field Museum in Chicago, Brown explains that grinders modify plastic Lego bricks. "There are electrical engineers who solder sensor arrays onto pieces and make very complex stuff, but to me that seems like the tail wagging the dog," says Brown, a 37-year-old naturalized American with a crisp British accent. "The coolness factor comes from having to live by the constraints of the blocks. It's like building in nanotech, except on a very large scale."

One of the top Lego builders in the world, Brown's most famous creation is 2001's Cube Solver, the first robot to finish the Rubik's Cube puzzle. When you place a messed-up cube in the Lego bot's rubber grippers, its optical sensors signal the color values to the central processor, or "RCX" in Lego-speak. Brown programmed algorithms for making cube moves in a hacked Lego programming language called NQC, or Not Quite C. The grippers twist the cube for the next move, and solve the puzzle in about ten minutes. More recently, Brown snapped together a pair of Lego hands that juggle three balls for up to two minutes — until latency in the Lego circuits causes the machine to fail.

But the Lego tinkerer's current project may be his toughest to date: designing a robot that can fold and throw a paper airplane. "I have about a ream of paper spread all over our house," says Brown. So far, he's figured out a way to get a crisp fold by running two rubber tires back and forth along the paper's edge. His device can complete an efficient aircraft (Brown sought advice from the *The Guinness Book of Records'* holder for longest flying paper airplane), but he has yet to find an elegant launch mechanism. "It's like object-oriented software: you break down a complex job into simpler individual processes and go from there." —*Bob Parks*

≫ **Serious Lego:** *jpbrown.i8.com*

Beer Blanket

Three years ago, after a bash at his apartment, **Adam Hunnell** was stuck trying to figure out what to do with a keg full of warm beer. "If you don't drink it all, it just gets ruined and you have to throw it out," says 23-year-old Hunnell, a grad student in the physics department at Pennsylvania's Case Western University. Not one to cry into his glass, though, the budding inventor drew up plans for a thermoelectric blanket that would keep kegs to a chilly 32 - 35 degrees F. In April 2004, he won $20,000 from the National Collegiate Inventors and Innovators Alliance to build the prototype.

The solid-state technology uses the Peltier effect, in which heat moves across two metal junctions when current flows through them. Hunnell's wrap will house 8 - 10 semiconductor plates, most likely made from bismuth telluride. Used to cool laser equipment, the components create a heat flux in one direction. And there may be other benefits to the Peltier effect: while one side of the material gets cold, the other side gets proportionally warmer. Nachos anyone? —*Bob Parks*

≫ **Keg Wrap:** *case.edu/news/2004/4-04/keg.htm*

Computing Gear

Some prefer a nuts-and-bolts approach to computing — like **Tim Robinson**, who built a version of Charles Babbage's Difference Engine No. 1 entirely out of Meccano parts. Babbage's original invention, which he partially prototyped in 1832 but didn't finish, proved that machines could generate polynomial solution tables. Meccano sets arrived later; the building toys hit it big in the 1920s and retain a worldwide following today, complete with regional building clubs, conventions, a mailing list, and the glossy magazine *Constructor Quarterly*.

Porting Meccano's assortment of trusses and gears to decimal computation took ingenuity. Robinson devised his basic counters by meshing 95-tooth wheels against 57-tooth wheels. The resulting 5:3 ratio means each small wheel-stop corresponds to a $\frac{1}{10}$ turn of the larger wheel. A rotating handle on top provides the power to Robinson's Difference Engine #1, which cranks out new solutions, literally, about every four seconds. As Robinson suggests, had Babbage had Meccano, the history of computing might be very different. —*Paul Spinrad*

≫ **Meccano Computing Machinery:** *meccano.us*

Touch and Go

If you've ever watched a child play with a pinstriped, pint-sized Hot Wheels racer, you may have wondered if the toy car was following some secret, virtual map in that child's mind. Sketch-a-Move not only proves that the answer is yes, it brings those invisible maps to life.

Created by London-based designers **Louise Klinker** and **Anab Jain** as a concept project for Mattel Hot Wheels, Sketch-a-Move allows you to use an erasable whiteboard marker to draw a line on the roof of a toy car — and as soon as you set it down, the car follows that path as a driving command. Draw a straight line, a spiral, a circle, or a squiggle, and the vehicle cruises or careens accordingly. Draw and redraw as many times as you desire. Klinker says she pursued the experiment "to challenge the intuitive and creative skills of children," and "to explore the unique relationships between small surface doodles and actual physical movements."

The prototype developed by Klinker and Jain was a non-fuctioning mock-up, but the technology necessary to make it work is in the here and now. By putting a touch-sensitive screen on the toy car's roof and placing a writeable surface over it, a microprocessor can read the stylus-like input — the line doodles — and translate it into movements performed by two solenoids and a motor, to steer and lend speed. A rechargeable battery powers the entire unit.

Sketch-a-Move's masterminds say initial presentations at Hot Wheels Headquarters were a hit. Still, no word yet on when the doodle-driven gizmos will show up on store shelves. —*Xeni Jardin*

Left: Sketch-a-Move performs a fancy slalom maneuver through styrofoam cups and around a toy robot.

≫ **Sketch-a-Move:** *lwk.dk/sketch_a_move/sketch_content.html*

Photography by Anab Jain and Louise Klinker

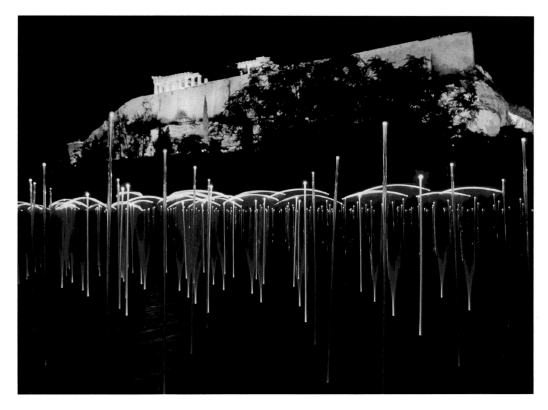

White Light / White Heat

Wheat fields rippled below the Acropolis once more last summer, as **Meejin Yoon's** installation played out at its foot. One of nine temporary installations commissioned for the 2004 Olympics, "White Noise/White Light" is a hi-tech re-visioning of agrarian bliss. An assistant professor in the architecture department at MIT and founder of MY Studio, Yoon pursued the commission because she wanted "to explore sound that was somehow filtered and transformed." She hit on the idea of white noise "out of thin air," and then decided to couple it with its visual equivalent, white light.

This was no ordinary sound and light show, however. The white lights were LEDs; the white noise was created based on a physical phenomenon called Johnson noise, which is generated by the thermal motions of electrons in a resistor. The noise was amplified by a factor of 100 million to produce the sound for the piece. Yoon and her team installed approximately 500 stalks of chest-high, semi-flexible, fiber-optic strands arranged in a grid; at the base of each stalk was a unit containing a speaker, a passive infrared sensor, and a microprocessor using a software differentiation algorithm to register heat and movement. As pedestrians walked through the field, they left a wake of sound and light.

The highlight, says Matthew Reynolds, an engineer/manager involved in the project, "came from watching literally hundreds of faces pressed against the fence as we tuned the installation for opening night, asking us (usually in Greek), 'Can we come in and play?'" —*Arwen O'Reilly*

≫ **Meejin Yoon:** *architecture.mit.edu/people/bg/cvyoon.html*

Cory Doctorow

HACKING THE DOG

Who says you have to spend thousands of dollars to get a cool robot? The world's toy stores brim with cheap-ass, rough-and-ready robotic platforms just begging to be modded.

NATALIE JEREMIJENKO, A YALE ENGINEERING professor, invented Feral Robot Dogs as a pedagogical exercise. Engineering profs would love to get their kids to build sophisticated bots like the Sony Aibo, but they're pricey as hell, and Sony has a history of threatening legal action against people who publish how-tos and code for hacking your Aibo.

Sony's Aibos are expensive toys, controlled from afar by the company's Attack Lawyers. Jeremijenko's dogs are cheap, out-of-control, and anything but toys.

Jeremijenko gives her students a selection of $20 toy dogs, the kind of thing that barks the national anthem or whizzes in circles, and asks her kids to take them to bits and divine what they can about the production design that went into the toys, to learn what they can about how mass-produced products are engineered.

Now the fun begins. First, the robots are modded with new drivetrains and fat wheels for rugged off-roading. Next, the students select sensors for their dogs: the sensor of choice is a Volatile Organic Compound (VOC) sniffer that can be had for a few dollars. VOCs are highly toxic chemicals released in urban environments by dry cleaners, power plants, and other polluters. The VOC sensors are the "noses" for the students' dogs, and they're connected to "brains" — low-cost programmable interrupt controllers that are configured to follow concentration gradients from the sensors, steering the dogs toward ever-higher levels of pollutants.

Once a pack of dogs is ready, Jeremijenko and students repair to a site suspected of containing VOCs. One such site was the Bronx's Starlight Park, which had been converted to a park after serving as a conEdison industrial site. The EPA had done a soil survey and given the park a clean

bill, but the Feral Dogs told another story: once released onto the turf, the dogs quickly converged on several toxic hotspots the Feds had missed.

Not surprising, really, since Feral Robot Dogs sample every 6cm, while the EPA's patented Guy-with-a-Clipboard method is accurate to 4m. What's more, the Robot Dogs have the quality Jeremijenko calls "legibility" — an unskilled person can examine their behavior and read it, understanding that the spot where all the robots have

"The EPA gave the park a clean bill, but the Feral Dogs quickly converged on several toxic hotspots the Feds had missed."

converged is the spot with the invisible, deadly toxic waste. Compare this with the EPA's method, in which the numbers on the clipboard and their interpretation are strictly the domain of experts, and the rest of us can only rely on their assurances that all is well.

The Feral Robotics movement is thriving, and its web hub (*xdesign.eng.yale.edu/feralrobots*) teems with how-tos and information on sourcing parts, contributed by Feral Roboticists around the world. Get modding!

Cory Doctorow (*craphound.com*) is European Affairs Co-ordinator for the Electronic Frontier Foundation (*eff.org*), a co-editor at Boing Boing (*boingboing.net*), and an award-winning science fiction writer (*craphound.com/est*). He lives in London, England.

Maker

Welcome to the Fab Lab >>

Interview by
D.C. Denison

Photography by
Emily Nathan

"The next revolution is going to be the personalization of fabrication."

Hi, I'm Neil Gershenfeld. I direct the Center for Bits and Atoms at MIT.

I'm going to take you on a tour of our Boston fab lab, at the South End Technology Center (SETC). The name fab lab can be interpreted two ways: a lab for fabrication, or simply a fabulous laboratory. This lab is one of a growing network of field labs we've set up since 2002, in places like rural India, northern Norway, Costa Rica, and Ghana.

These labs grew out of work on campus at Massachusetts Institute of Technology where we have been doing basic research on additive digital fabrication. The idea that inspires us is that the next revolution is going to be the personalization of manufacturing: using accessible digital technology and machine tools to program the physical world we live in, just as we today program the bits in worlds of information. To do this research, we bought millions of dollars worth of machinery at MIT. My colleagues and I started teaching a course modestly titled "How to Make (almost) Anything" to teach students how to use these machines. The interest in the course was overwhelming. What was also surprising were the wonderfully quirky ways students used the tools, using the technology as a means of personal expression, which I believe is entirely analogous to the earlier personalization of computation.

Intrigued by this parallel, with support from the National Science Foundation, we began setting up prototype versions of these capabilities in the field. We wanted to see how personal fabricators will eventually be used. You can think of a fab lab as being comparable to the minicomputer stage in the history of computing; DEC PDPs were used by workgroups rather than individuals, but that was good enough for inventing most of the modern applications of computers.

By personal fabrication, I mean a desktop machine that can create three-dimensional structures as well as logic, sensing, acutation, and display. The kind of research we're doing at MIT will eventually lead to those capabilities being integrated into a single process.

Let's look around. >> >>

Maker

Today, the fab lab is a collection of components, but you could think of it as one big machine. The fab lab isn't a static thing; bit by bit, we're starting to use the machines to make the machines, until a lab can eventually make another lab.

The fab lab comprises about $25,000 in equipment, consumables, and software. Currently, there's a laser cutter that makes 2D and 3D structures, a sign cutter that plots in copper to make antennas and flex circuits, a high-resolution milling machine that makes circuit boards and precision parts, and programming tools for low-cost, high-speed, tiny microcontrollers.

A laser cutter is a bit like a laser printer, but the laser is so powerful that it can cut through materials. And the beam can be placed with a resolution of a thousandth of an inch (a mil), which is good enough to cut out two-dimensional parts that snap together to assemble three-dimensional structures. Right now, that's faster and cheaper than printing in 3D.

The machines in the lab come with programs that contain strong assumptions about how they're going to be used: 2D shapes on the laser cutter, signs on the sign cutter. So one of the first things I had to do for the fab labs was write a CAM (computer-aided manufacturing) program that could read all the different kinds of ways that people describe things, and turn them into toolpaths for all the different ways it's possible to make them. Another program helps users share their files and experiences as they work, so that users can teach each other rather than relying on a fixed curriculum.

Once we started taking these things into the field, we quickly found that there's an instrumentation and fabrication divide that's even bigger than the digital divide — a desktop computer isn't much use if you don't have a desk. One fab lab in India is working on sensors for agriculture and health care, another on crafts for rural artisans. The Ghanian lab is working on solar energy conversion and wireless networks. In Boston, a group of girls at SETC set up the laser cutter on a street corner and held a high-tech craft sale, making things on demand from scrap materials. They also made $100 in an afternoon, a life-changing experience in a community with limited economic opportunities for them.

A group of students from MIT's Black Students' Union working with the laser cutter.

Maker

I'm going to demonstrate how we make a circuit board in the fab lab.

1. We'll start with a schematic of a circuit board that was designed at the Ghana lab. We call this design an "Efe," which in Ghanian means "it's beautiful." This circuit board has a proximity sensor and an LED, and it can communicate with a computer.

2. We make circuits boards in the fab labs by machining rather than the more conventional process of chemical etching, because the solutions used for etching produce nasty chemical waste. The tabletop milling machine we use has metrology good to a tenth of a mil, which along with ¹⁄₆₄" end-mills makes it possible to make circuit boards with the pitch of fine surface-mount components.

3. Ed Baafi from SETC is "stuffing" the circuit board. Surface-mount circuit boards are usually assembled by "pick and place" machines because of the resolution needed to align the parts. What enables us to do it by hand is a trick based on surface tension. Molten solder prefers to be on the hot traces, not on the cold places in between, so if you get the part and solder close enough, they'll all end up in the right place. These circuit boards use microcontrollers from Atmel that can cost less than a dollar. But they can run faster than a million instructions a second, which makes it possible to implement things like communication modulation, video drivers, and sensor signal chains in software. Together, the milling machine and microcontroller make microns and microseconds accessible to the masses.

4. We're programming the chip to instruct it how to read the sensor, drive the LED, and interface with a computer. Instead of using dedicated programming hardware, a cable is used from a parallel port to generate the signals required for in-circuit programming. A serial port is used for power and communications.

5. "Hello World" is the first program one usually writes when learning a new programming language. We've adapted it to say "Hello Make."

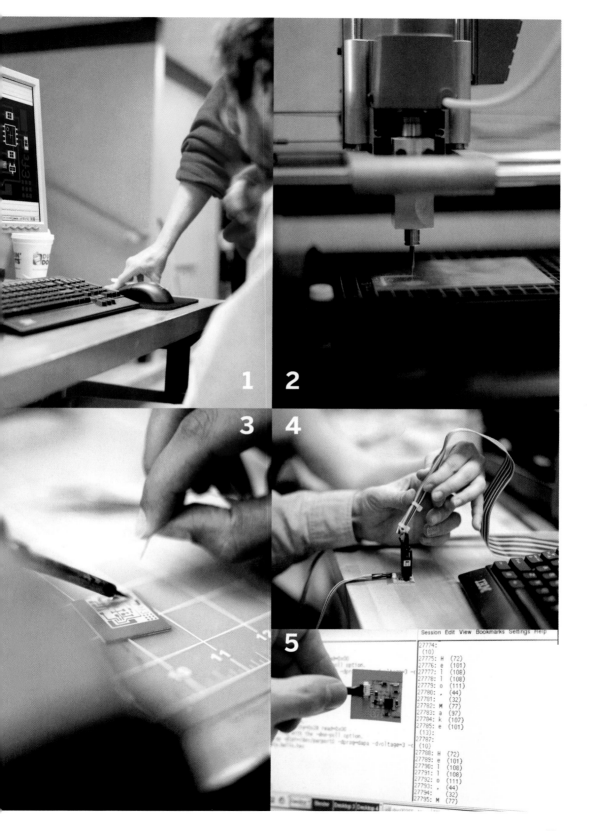

1

2

3

4

5

Session Edit View Bookmarks Settings Help

```
27774:
 (10)
27775: H  (72)
27776: e  (101)
27777: l  (108)
27778: l  (108)
27779: o  (111)
27780: .  (44)
27781:    (32)
27782: M  (77)
27783: a  (97)
27784: k  (107)
27785: e  (101)
 (13):
27787:
 (10)
27788: H  (72)
27789: e  (101)
27790: l  (108)
27791: l  (108)
27792: o  (111)
27793: .  (44)
27794:    (32)
27795: M  (77)
```

Maker

Many projects in the fab lab start not with a CAD drawing but with a model or a sketch.

1. Amon Millner is holding a sketch drawn that morning. This gets scanned into a computer and can then be output on any of the machines.

2. A lasercut-foam version of me. This is a powerful approach to engineering design, pioneered by architect Frank Gehry. We convert something made in one material (that's easy to work with) to another material that's matched to an application.

The same sketch could have been plotted on the sign cutter to make a sticker. If a copper foil is used instead of vinyl, then the sign cutter can be used to make flexible circuits. Because they're still stickers, they can be stuck onto anything else, like a piece of cardboard for functional jewelry.

While there are many years of research to come on molecular digital fabrication, we're already finding clear answers to our original questions about the applications of personal fabrication.

In the developed world, people can create things they want rather than need, meeting markets as small as one person. And in the developing world, it's the local solution to local technological needs, bringing IT development, rather than just IT, to the masses.

Along the way, we're finding the same kind of response in the field that we saw at MIT. Kids come off the street, in Boston or Ghana, and refuse to leave until they get their projects working. Most gratifying of all for me is the growing collaboration across the labs, seeing Norwegians from far above the Arctic Circle working with counterparts from inner-city Boston on the design of their wireless network antennas.

Recipe for a Fab Lab

Here are some of the essential machines, excluding computers, that you'd need to build a fab lab. For a complete inventory, see *fab.cba.mit.edu/fab/inv.html.*

Laser Cutter
Epilog Mini 24X12
$19,900
www.epiloglaser.com

Vinyl Cutter
Roland CX-24
$2,295
www.rolanddga.com

Heat Gun
Weller 6966C
$138.65
www.techni-tool.com
www.amazon.com

Dustbuster
Black and Decker CHV9600
$29.99
www.amazon.com

NC Milling Machine
Roland MDX-20
$4,495
www.rolanddga.com

Oscilloscope
Tektronix TDS1002
$995
www.techni-tool.com
www.amazon.com

Variable Speed Scroll Saw
DeWalt DW7885 20"
$449.99
www.amazon.com

Maker

How to Make (almost) Anything

MAKE sent photographer Carlin Wing to the lab at MIT where students were showing the work they had created in the class in the fall semester. Gershenfeld teaches a three-hour class once a week. The TAs (Raffi Krikorian and Manu Prakash) and shop technician John DiFrancesco spend the rest of the week, weekend, and nights with the students to help them build and put the ideas into practice. Krikorian told us about the projects.

1. Sergio Araya and Ayah Bdeir's Wall. Sergio and Ayah are setting up their project. They wanted to make a wall surface that could be programmed to set patterns into the wall. The sheet in front of the wall would dance with those patterns.

2. Anmol Madan's Wireless Wearable. Anmol wanted to integrate accelerometers and Bluetooth GSR (Galvanic Skin Response) sensors so he could feed that information into a computer and have it know how you were "feeling" at the time. He's exploring affective computing applications to understand how people react under stress during a negotiation or on a date.

3. Gerardo Perez and Han Hoang's Robot. Gerardo and Han built a macroscale pick-and-place machine. They wanted to build a robot that could assemble structures larger than itself.

4. Vincent Leclerc's Volumetric Display. Vincent's display was a 2D grid of LEDs that he spun around very quickly. By controlling when the LEDs go on and off, and relying on persistence of vision, the display looks like an object floating in the air.

5. John Harrison's Microphone. John's showing off a project he did during one of the weekly assignments. He rigged up a microphone with ultrasonic sensors so he could tell how far away the speaker was from the microphone and automatically adjust the gain.

6. Christine Liu's Jellyfish. Christine made a jellyfish that reacts as you approach it, shaking its tentacles and glowing while making a zapping sound. When left alone, this device undulates like a jellyfish does.

7. Amon Millner's Claytroller. Amon wanted to create an easy way for children to build their own video game controllers. He envisioned a system of blocks that you could assemble, and the bricks would then coordinate to relay their input data to the video game system.

For more information on the 2004 fall class and the rest of its projects, visit *fab.cba.mit.edu/classes/863.04*.

For more information on people, projects, and processes, Neil Gershenfeld's book on personal fabrication, *Fab*, will be published in April by Basic Books.

GLOWSTICK A GO-GO

Bunnie Huang prototypes two kinetic glowsticks.

Glowsticking emerged out of the techno club scene, which features bone-rattling riffs and vicious grooves. Dancers whirled a pair of glowsticks to trace out beautiful, curvaceous patterns and Lissajous figures in the dark of the dance floors.

When high-efficiency LEDs became available, so-called "photon lights" (high-intensity keychain fob LEDs) were used in place of the glowsticks. Eventually, these photon lights became available at carnivals, fairs, clubs, and raves. Moving forever forward, the photon lights evolved to include multi-color LEDs that would sequence through a series of colors, thus tracing a multi-colored path through the dark as the light was swung around.

I've always been a big fan of electronic music of all kinds, starting with Information Society and Kraftwerk back in the '80s. While I was at a party watching glowsticking dancers, I got to thinking. What if, instead of creating a single arc of light, the dancers could create whole, two-dimensional patterns of light as they danced? So inspired, I began to hack my own "kinetic glowstick."

Since I wanted a ribbon of light with a visible pattern in it, I could not use just a single LED like the photon lights. The device had to contain a row of LEDs that would flash with a preprogrammed and pre-timed pattern. This pattern would then smear out in the viewer's eyes and create the illusion of a solid, 2D pattern in the air.

The requirements for a Kinetic Glowstick:
* A row of LEDs
* A sequencer to control the rate and pattern of flashing of the LEDs
* A memory store to contain all the LED patterns
* A power source

The sequencer will pull "sprites" from the memory store and relay them to the LEDs. A sprite is jargon from computer graphics for a 2D array of pixels that define an image for use in animations. Many of our old favorite video games, such as Galaga and Pac-Man, use sprites for animation. The number and resolution of the sprites stored in memory will define the richness and variety of images seen by the viewers.

The Back-of-the-Hand Prototype

When I start a project, I usually look around for a few spare parts. This prototype began with a circuit board I had built a long time ago for a class that I taught at MIT. The board had a single Xilinx "Spartan" FPGA connected to a row of 16 LEDs — a perfect starting point. The board also had an on-board serial ROM socket for configuring the FPGA

Flash Dancing

Why do we perceive a path of light when a dancer moves flashing lights in the dark? That's "persistence of vision." Our eyes and brain continue to see a light for 15 to 30 milliseconds (ms) after it has gone out. An image that updates once every 15 ms updates at a rate of 66Hz (frequency is the reciprocal of period). It's no mistake that AC power uses 60Hz to eliminate any flicker from light bulbs.

You may also notice this effect when setting your monitor's refresh rate. Another example is the Fantazein™ clock; it employs a bar of LEDs swinging on an inverted pendulum to trace out digits that appear to float mysteriously in thin air.

Figure 1: A dancer swinging a kinetic glowstick on each arm creates two different patterns of light.

FPGA Primer

An FPGA (Field Programmable Gate Array) is an integrated circuit found in all kinds of hardware products, from IP routers to MP3 players. They are used to implement highly integrated, custom digital circuits as a low-risk, low-NRE (non-recurring engineering charges — the upfront engineering effort required to make a product) alternative to full-custom silicon designs.

A gate array is a custom chip fabricated in two stages: a set of generic transistor patterns is first put down, and a set of interconnects is added later on by the customer. Transistors are expensive to design; making a generic starting base for devices helps many small customers leverage economies of scale. "Field programmable" describes a device programmed "in the field" by the customer. The FPGA I've chosen for this project uses metal interconnects connected via switches, each driven by 1-bit memory cells.

"ring oscillator" as a frequency source. A ring oscillator uses a chain of inverters looped onto itself to create an unstable system that oscillates. Such a ring oscillator can be easily implemented inside an FPGA with no external components by configuring the FPGA to wire a chain of inverting functions together in a ring topology.

The second problem I had to solve was the need for regulated power. All digital circuits are happiest when they have a nice, solid flow of DC current through them. The little board that I had lying around had no onboard capability to regulate the power input. Connecting a battery directly to the board would not be a very robust solution because a battery's output voltage will vary by as much as 50 percent over its operational life.

So I had to add some kind of voltage regulator to the prototype. We will discuss the specifics of the voltage regulator implementation later; for now, let's return to thinking about the more interesting problem of how to drive the LEDs with the desired flashing patterns.

in standalone applications. There were a few other features in the board, but they could be ignored for this project.

There were two problems I had to solve. First, there was no onboard oscillator. All conventional digital circuits require a source of timing to drive the rate of computation. The source of this timing is often generically referred to as an oscillator. In many applications, a precisely cut piece of quartz crystal is used, and the mechanical vibrations (or oscillations, if you will) of the crystal are used as the source of timing. However, this board had no such thing built into it, since it was intended to be used as part of a much larger system.

The easiest way around this problem is to use a

 et's take a look at the FPGA, illustrated in Figure 2. This configuration provides us with the ability to show up to 16 different sprites, and each sprite can be as large as 32x16 pixels. Let's see how this works in detail.

The heart of the device is a 512x16-bit ROM. Each ROM output bit drives an LED. The address bits to the ROM (nine address bits allows us to access up to $2^9 = 512$ locations) are split into two logical banks, a "frame count" and a "sprite count." The ring oscillator's output, which runs at a nominal frequency of 16kHz, is used to drive a 24-bit counter.

Before discussing how the counter is connected to the sprite ROM, let's first review a few interesting properties about binary counters. The first is that each successively significant bit of a counter toggles at a rate equal to exactly one half of the previous bit.

Figure 2: Block diagram of the FPGA internals used in the first prototype. The large box around the three leftmost elements indicates the boundary of the FPGA.

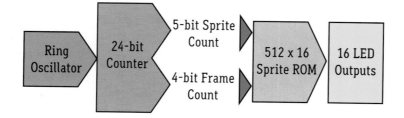

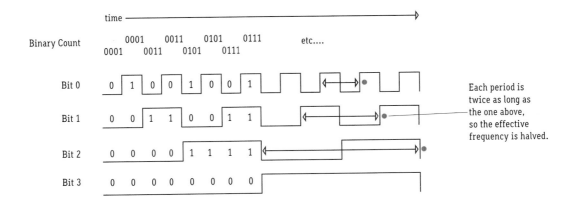

Figure 3: Controlling frequency with a binary counter.

This effect is evident if you look at the numbers 0 through 7 written out in binary, as illustrated above in Figure 3.

Notice how the frequency of the binary pattern reduces by ½ as you go from the top row to the bottom row. In other words, the digits in the top row toggle between one and zero; the digits in the second row toggle half as frequently as in the first; and so on. This shows how a binary counter inherently performs a divide-by-two in frequency function. The second interesting property of a binary counter, which is not so remarkable, is that when a binary counter gets to its highest count, it wraps around to zero again.

Thus, when driving the address bits of the sprite ROM, what we are really interested in is the frequency at which the bits are sequenced. Going through all the bits at a rate equal to the base rate of the ring oscillator is too fast; at 16kHz, the pattern will be very tight, and in fact, it's unlikely that a viewer will see any pattern at all. Recall that we really want an update rate equal to roughly 30Hz.

In other words, we want a sprite to be fully "displayed" around 30 times a second. Going back to the frequency divider property of a binary counter, we see that bit 9 on a counter clocked at 16kHz will have a toggle rate roughly equal to 15 times a second. So, we wire bits 5 through 9 of the counter to drive the "sprite count" address input of the ROM. If I wanted an update rate of strictly 30 times a second, I would have used bit 8 of the counter. But in perceptual tests of the circuit that I conducted, I found that the pattern looked best at a rate of 15Hz, slightly below the threshold of persistence of vision.

Recall that one of the goals was to provide a 32x16-bit sprite pattern. This means that a 5-bit (e.g. $2^5 = 32$) counter was all I needed for the sprite pattern counter. Bits 16 through 19 are used to drive the "frame count" input for the ROM. These four bits are used to choose which sprite is looped into the LEDs, up to a total of 16 different patterns. Again, recall that the binary counter also serves as

continued on page 186

Ring Around the Rosy

To visualize how a ring oscillator works, imagine you have some people standing in a circle holding hands. Each person will try to raise his or her left hand if the right hand is lowered, and vice versa. If you have two people holding hands, then one person will raise one hand and the other will lower one hand; after this point, the system stops (this is actually how many basic memory cells are built, using a pair of inverters tied together in a loop).

However, if you had three people in such a ring, and each of them were to try and raise their hands in opposing polarities, you would find that there is no steady state: hands will go up and down at roughly three times the rate it takes for a single person to raise or lower his or her hand. Thus, for every loop with an odd number of people, you will encounter a resonance or oscillatory effect, and the period of the oscillation around the loop increases as you add more people to the ring.

In circuits, we build such rings out of long chains of inverters to make a quick and dirty frequency source. Such frequency sources are far from stable or ideal because the rate at which an inverter can switch depends upon the temperature, voltage, and particular structural defects within that inverter.

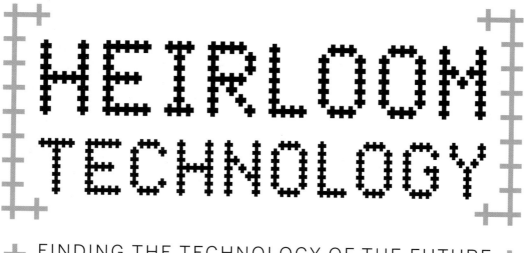

HEIRLOOM TECHNOLOGY

FINDING THE TECHNOLOGY OF THE FUTURE FROM THE FORGOTTEN IDEAS OF THE PAST

very once in a while, I find that I've wasted years of my life on some problem only to discover that the solution already exists. Reinventing the wheel. The "not invented here" syndrome. My granddad would have called it "ignorance," "stupidity," or "vast undertakings with half-vast ideas." It's a lot easier to spot when other people are doing it. One of these other people once told me with pride, "We do our research in the lab, not the library." I just saw the remains of their machine sitting in a hallway.

It took 15 geniuses (tested) 15 years (sleep-deprived) to finish. Not only can't they give away their machine, they'll have to pay someone to dispose of it. A little time in the library could have saved them all that effort just to poison a landfill at great expense.

Choosing the right problem is, of course, at least as important as how to solve it. So I'll let the experts pick a few problems, and then I'll try to find heirloom-technology solutions.

Photograph courtesy of Getty Images

PROBLEM

Efi Arazi, the richest Israeli in the world, once said to me, "I'm looking for something to make the old man's package stand up!"

Judging from the quantity of unsolicited email I get on this subject, he's not alone. I did a little reading, and the causes of the problem include bicycles. It turns out those tiny little racing seats crush your pudendal nerve, causing impotence in both men and women. The hard-bodies in the spandex with the logos and funny shoes are sexual cripples with numb crotches.

HEIRLOOM SOLUTION:

Manufacture a bicycle seat with a deep groove down the middle.

There's one that's more than 100 years old in the Wright brothers' bicycle shop, now located at Greenfield Village in Dearborn, Michigan. The Wright brothers' airplanes aren't very good, but their bicycle seats are incredible. This one predates modern research by 100 years, and with a little DayGlo spray paint, it would look great on any modern bicycle. I wonder how many millions of people saw it in the theme park before someone realized what it was for and put copies of it back on the market. It probably had to be reinvented from scratch, at a human cost of thousands of sexually debilitated bicyclists. The problem is serious, hasn't changed for a hundred years, and this simple, effective solution was once well known. Perhaps no one read what the Wrights and others had to say about this seat, or they were unable to understand it due to changes in the language. This is an example of how easy it can be to lose an heirloom technology, even when conditions seem very favorable for its preservation.

The Wright's engine is excellent — as good as a modern engine in terms of fuel efficiency and power-to-weight ratio. When I say the Wright flyers are bad, I mean they're dangerous and hard to fly. The Wright brothers made a mistake with their wind tunnel: they set the airspeed over their model wings to the same scale as that of the model. Due to the nonlinear behavior of fluid flows, they were actually optimizing their wing shape for supersonic flight.

All their famous wind-tunnel work ended up producing a wing that is too flat, produces little lift, and is prone to stall. The Wright brothers' wing is worse, in fact, than what they started with: the bird-wing sections measured by Otto Lilienthal, who built larger model wings than the Wrights, so his errors of scale were less significant.

In this example of technology decay, belief in a flawed scientific theory leads a series of brilliant researchers to start with something nearly perfect and create something barely usable. Frank Bethwaite, an Australian planing dinghy wizard, told me this proverb: "Model tests are good, and the larger the model, the better they are. Full-scale models are best of all." In many cases, the disputed scale factors are more significant than actual tunnel test data — one reason many modern airplanes are built and tested full scale, without any tunnel tests at all. Bird-wing sections should be included in the standard catalogs of foil sections. I expect breakthroughs in aerodynamics to come from this ancient, pre-human heirloom technology: the highly evolved shapes of birds' wings. We are far from understanding them, but we don't need to fully understand them to use them.

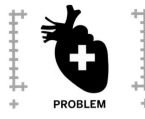

2.4 million Americans die
of disease every year.

iopharm is a great field to be in. All your market research is done for you for free by the CDC (United States Department of Health and Human Services Centers for Disease Control and Prevention). It consists of counting the sick people and what they die of. Cardiovascular disease is number one at almost a million per year in the U.S. It's caused by atherosclerosis — fat deposits in the blood vessels that eventually block the blood flow enough to cause a heart attack or stroke. Atherosclerosis is caused by too much food and too little exercise. Take a bite of your snack and consider this article a form of assisted suicide.

HEIRLOOM SOLUTION 1:
Live by hunting, the oldest of all human technologies.

Recent bestsellers *The Zone*, *Protein Power*, and *Dr. Atkins' Diet Revolution* make carbohydrates the culprit in heart disease. It seems humans have not yet adapted to the change from the protein-and-fat-rich diet of the hunter to the carbohydrate-rich diet of the farmer. Hunter-gatherers as a rule have no heart disease, diabetes, or tooth decay. The exceptions are those who consume abundant carbohydrates.

HEIRLOOM SOLUTION 2:
Eat an 800-calorie diet for several weeks.

Read *Hunger Disease*, written by the Jewish doctors of the Warsaw Ghetto prior to the exterminations of 1942. This work chronicles the terrible effects of a starvation diet. The first phase is surprising: "Disappearance of surplus fat. This stage was reminiscent of the time before the war when people went to Marienbad, Karlsbad, or Vichy for a reducing cure and came back looking younger and feeling better." (*Hunger Disease*, ed M. Winick) The subsequent phases are all bad. But no trace of atherosclerosis was found in any autopsy.

This book is a true heirloom. These scientists literally died to give us not only a moving work of literature, but data that could help save our own lives. We owe it to ourselves and to them to make good use of it. Fasting/controlled starvation needs further research to be understood as a treatment. Oprah Winfrey (a diet victim) and Steve Callahan (a lifeboat survivor and author of *Adrift*) have experienced one hazard, which is that the body responds to starvation by reducing its metabolism for a long time, leading to rapid fat buildups when food intake is increased.

HEIRLOOM SOLUTION 3:
Establish and obey taboos.

Declare that overeating (gluttony) and lack of exercise (sloth) are bad (sins, taboo) and will eventually kill you (deadly). Decathlon winner Bruce Jenner, the Surgeon General, and innumerable others have tried this approach with disappointing results. However, when practiced as part of a complete program (orders) in a supportive community (monastery), it can be more effective. Such authors as John Cassian (c. 360 - 435 A.D.) and Augustine of Hippo (354 - 371 A.D.) claim success. According to the CDC, these "deadly sins" are the leading causes of death, especially if you include the alcohol fatalities under Gluttony and the firearm deaths under Anger. Tobacco is the major killer after gluttony and sloth, and some sects have responded by making it taboo as well. (Tobacco couldn't have been in the original list of sins, because Christians didn't encounter it until Columbus.)

Maker   Tim Anderson

PROBLEM

Tropical diseases spread
rapidly and unnecessarily.

This winter I lived in the beautiful town of Jayapura on the north coast of Papua. That's the Indonesian half of the island of New Guinea. Most of the people I met had contracted malaria multiple times. Some had multiple strains simultaneously. My girlfriend and I avoided malaria by taking Malarone, an expensive antimalarial drug. The Indonesian government encourages people to move to Papua from more densely populated islands. They bring customs unknown to the native Papuans, such as defecating in the river and bathing in it, and building houses surrounded with drainage gutters. These gutters contain stagnant water full of mosquitoes. The mosquitoes fly back and forth at night, spreading malaria, dengue, filariasis, etc., from one person to another.

The tidiness of the houses and yards makes it hard to see how hazardous the place really is. When I realized what was going on, I felt trapped and terrified, not to mention my body ached. I had fevers and chills that came and went, and a bright-red blotchy rash all over my body. It turned out that I'd contracted the parasite schistosomiasis (AKA bilharzia) by stepping in a stream of water. I'd barely recovered some strength when my girlfriend, Michelle, came down with dengue. We couldn't even escape because we'd left our passports with an immigration official to renew our visas; he was hospitalized with cerebral malaria, and no one else in the office could open the safe.

Well, life goes on — as long as you don't die. A local friend took me to visit a native Papuan stilt village in the harbor. It's known as "Vietnam Village" because the residents

don't allow the police there. It's clean, but somewhat weathered and impoverished-looking, like most stilt villages. Then the genius of its design hit me....

HEIRLOOM SOLUTION:
Build a saltwater stilt village.

The houses are surrounded by saltwater, so there's no place for mosquitoes to breed. The Anopheles mosquito that carries Malaria rarely flies more than 100 meters in a night. The village is further than that from any standing, fresh water. There's a breeze from the ocean that blows any bugs away and keeps the temperature comfortable. Even if dengue mosquitoes could live in saltwater, they wouldn't enter the houses, because they're poor fliers and don't go above about six feet. Few, if any, waterborne diseases are carried by salt water. This was the healthiest place in the city! In fact, healthier than any neighborhood I'd seen in the U.S. The people there live by fishing. The men spend their time working out paddling canoes and fishing, and they consume a fresh, high-protein diet. Many are built like Olympic athletes. It turned out that several were, in fact, Olympic athletes who had won medals in rowing. Their wealth of heirloom technology is impressive. Herbal remedies, giant canoes that carry dozens of people at high speed through rough water, fishing techniques, epic songs about their history with the Dutch queen.... They value their knowledge, and even have ceremonies involving particular herbs to officially pass on a skill or talent to a chosen successor.

GETTING STARTED IN HEIRLOOM TECHNOLOGY

Where to start? Since it's all about passing on things of value, how about getting your kids into it? The following were my favorites when I was growing up. I learned a lot about how to build things from these books. I'm listing them in approximate order of difficulty. A child who can handle a pocketknife or sew is old enough. Some of the books are out of print. To find out-of-print books, search on *abe.com*, Amazon, eBay, and at libraries. To find other sources, look up *abe.com* on *alexa.com*, a web information service.

BOOK LIST:

Wilder, James Austin. Jack-Knife Cookery. New York: E.P. Dutton & Co., 1929. 186 pages illus., 20 cm. Intended for children. The cutest little book ever made. How to cook without utensils and camp without carrying much. Maybe the first book on ultralight camping. The author traveled all over the world studying traditional techniques. Then he tested them with his scout troop in Hawaii for years before writing this book. So the instructions are clear, easy to follow, and everything works. Full of cute, easy-to-understand line drawings. A lighthearted tome that will help you find the deserted island in your backyard.

Jaeger, Ellsworth. Wildwood Wisdom. New York: The Macmillan Company, 1945. 491 pages illus. 21 cm. Intended for children. Similar to the above but much thicker. Traditional regional, Eskimo, and Indian technology for young campers. Especially good for making your own winter clothing. Judging from what modern Eskimos wear, the mittens and boots are still better than anything you can buy. Profusely illustrated.

Beard, Daniel C. The American Boy's Handy Book: What to Do and How to Do It. New York: Charles Scribner's Sons, †1882. 391 pages illus., 2 fold. pl., 20 cm. Reissued by David R. Goodine publisher, 1998, 441 pages. Intended for children. A bestseller from 1882, beautifully illustrated and very appealing. From age 10 on, I spent years building projects from this book. My "Man Friday Raft" log raft sank immediately. My "Tom Thumb Iceboat" failed to move at all. I concluded that boys a hundred years ago were far more skilled than I. Now that I'm almost 40, it's obvious that my raft logs were too heavy and the iceboat blades were the wrong shape. Those masterful boys from the book must have had a lot of help from parents and grandparents. This book is good for that. Just be aware that some of the drawings are wrong and some important information is omitted. If you'd grown up in the 1840s around rafts and iceboats, you'd probably find it easier to fill in the blanks than I did. That said, you must have this book, and most public libraries already do.

Wigginton, Eliot, ed. The Foxfire Book: Hog dressing, log-cabin building, snake lore, mountain crafts and food, and other affairs of plain living. **New York: Anchor Press/**Doubleday, 1972. 384 pages illus., 24 cm. Produced by high-school students in Appalachian Georgia. They interview their relatives and neighbors to document traditional crafts, stories, and lore. My parents gave me this book for Christmas. I immediately saw what project I wanted to do. So my mom drove me out to a friend's farm to get a load of manure to make gunpowder. After leaching out the nitrates, I was in too much of a hurry to evaporate the water. I overheated the crystals, and whoosh! — a big mushroom cloud, as the mess all went off at once. Foxfire project is a giant success story: the kids learn academic skills and to value their heritage; the old people get to pass on their wealth of wisdom; and the rest of us get access to low-impact technology that's stood the test of time. Everything is good about the Foxfire project. Start one in your village.

Foxfire 2: Ghost stories, spinning and weaving, wagon making, midwifing, corn shuckin', and more.

Foxfire 3: Animal care, banjos and dulcimers, wild plant foods, butter churns, ginseng, and more.

Foxfire 4: Fiddle making, spring houses, horse trading, sassafras tea, berry buckets, gardening, and other affairs of plain living.

Foxfire 5: Ironmaking, blacksmithing, flintlock rifles, bear hunting, and other affairs of plain living.

Foxfire 6: Shoemaking, 100 toys and games, gourd banjos and song bows, wooden locks, a water-powered sawmill, and more.

Foxfire 7: Traditions of mountain religious heritage, covering ministers, revivals, baptisms, gospel singing, faith healing, camp meetings, snake handling, and more.

Foxfire 8: Southern folk pottery, from pug mills, ash glazes, and groundhog kilns, to face jugs, churns, and roosters, mule swapping, chicken fighting, and more.

Foxfire 9: Twentieth anniversary of the high school program. General stores, the Jud Nelson wagon, a praying rock, a Catawban Indian potter, haint tales, quilting, home cures, and the log cabin revisited.

Tim Anderson, founder of Z Corp., has a home at *stuff.mit.edu/people/robot/home.html*. When not ice-kite-butt-boarding in a rooster-crested motorcycle helmet, he can be found all over the world using and documenting heirloom technologies.

THE OPEN SOURCE CAR: A DESIGN BRIEF

The time is right for a true people's hybrid vehicle. By Saul Griffith

In his essay "In the Beginning Was the Command Line," Neil Stephenson uses a car metaphor to describe the various players in the operating system dilemma. Apple had "sleek Euro-style sedans"; Microsoft had "colossal station wagons"; and BeOS (now defunct) had "fully operational Batmobiles." And then there was Linux — "a tank ... of space-age materials and jammed with sophisticated technology" capable of 100mpg, reliable and robust, being given away for free.

Today, oil prices are rising. Demand for hybrid vehicles in the U.S. is higher than production. Can the last piece of Stephenson's metaphor be turned around? Is it worth contemplating an open source car?

On July 21, 2003, the last (old-style) VW Beetle was produced in Puebla, Mexico. It was car number 21,529,464. One of a host of incredibly successful cars with common features harking to their original "design briefs," the Beetle and its peers — the Citroen 2CV (3,872,583 cars made), Land Rover (2,400,000), Mini (5,250,000), Trabant (3,096,000), and Fiat 500 (3,678,000) — were utilitarian, efficient, maintainable, flexible, and the antithesis of the modern industry. The briefs were often charming: Boulanger (designer of the Citroen 2CV) was tasked with designing an "umbrella on four wheels" capable of getting two peasants and their 100Kg of farm goods to market at 60km/h

(and 78mpg!), traversing a ploughed field without breaking the eggs it was carrying.

While none of these vehicles were "open sourced," all of them endured any number of modifications and demonstrated modularity and flexibility in their lifetimes. Third-party industries arose to supply parts and modifications. This was taken to an extreme in the early 1960s when Bruce Meyers retrofitted a fiberglass body to a shortened VW chassis, giving birth to the "Manx" dune buggy. Only 7,000 Manxes were produced, but the phenom was so successful that nearly 300,000 clones were made worldwide. The vast majority were assembled and built with all types of modifications by end users.

After a 30-year hiatus, Meyers recently began producing dune buggy kits again. The new "Manxter 2+2" has improved safety features, but otherwise stays close to its Spartan and immensely fun roots. A "95 percent kit" is also now being offered to appeal to a time-short population that desires the fun of putting together a car without the attendant frustrations (and delights) of hacking it yourself. It is, in essence, a mail-order car: fill out a few web forms, bolt an engine in when it arrives a few weeks later, and drive away.

Other than this example, modern consumers accustomed to choice find that the auto industry doesn't offer much outside a bland mean. If you can

Maker

personalize your desktop, why not your car? A few savvy players like Mini and Scion are now offering the illusion of large choice via online ordering systems with "personalization" of body panel colors, wheels, stereo, and upholstery.

But why not go a lot further? Drive-by-wire technology, better electric motors, better batteries, within-hub motors, and (of course) hybrid concepts are changing the modularity of cars. The dominant architecture is up for challenge. Now you can choose your own optimal combination of gasoline engine and electric motor to tailor your hybrid to your driving style and conditions. Electro Automo-

The web is peppered with how-to sites for converting your old car into an electric vehicle, but why not develop SourceForge-style documentation for an open source hybrid?

tive (*electroauto.com*), founded in 1979 as a source for components to turn standard gasoline-burning cars into battery-powered electrics, will sell you a plugin (pun intended) electric conversion kit that, with minimal modifications, could bolt into the Manxter. (This could be the Red Hat of the bunch!) For $35,000 and minimal assembly, you'd be driving your own four-seat electric vehicle with a roll cage, 75mph-plus top speed, and 50-100mpg range. This might be the first electric vehicle you'd ever feel sexy in. Add one of the new, clean-burning, four-stroke engines found in snowmobiles and four-wheelers, and it'd be a long-range hybrid.

The web is peppered with how-to sites for converting your old car into an electric vehicle, but why not develop SourceForge-style documentation for an open source hybrid? Call the site opendesignhybrid.org, and publish the code for motor controllers and the CAD files for transmission-conversion parts. Annotate the demand for parts so multiple users can lower their individual costs by sharing tooling

overhead. In time, one can imagine cottage industries rising to support the project with custom parts, assembly services, Manxter-style bodies, interiors in many configurations, and complete parts kits.

There are millions of Americans tinkering with hotrods, antique autos, and old clunkers every day in this country. There are hugely popular TV shows inspiring these people: *Monster Garage, Orange County Choppers, American HotRod.* Want to see innovation in the hybrid electric automobile market? There's an R&D department composed of a million people in a million garages around the world. The digital tools for support are here: search Yahoo! Groups for auto-tech chat groups; eBay is a junkyard of parts; and eMachineShop and McMaster-Carr will deliver parts to your door.

A true people's car is doable. It just needs a Linus Torvalds (or maybe 20) and a user community. But before we throw down our Linux boxes to save the world with a publicly built 100mpg tank, here's the biggest catch: legislation and registration. Most kit cars fly under the radar because they are registered as the original vehicle of the chassis "donor." A recent Californian bill allows for "Special Construction" vehicles, but it's limited to 500 per year, and the demand already exceeds the allotment.

Unless a new, popular "donor" chassis is appropriated from industry, a group or organization would have to agree on a chassis/body and have it crash tested. This is an expensive process, BUT NOT IMPOSSIBLE.

There are, however, 21 million VWs still out there...

Saul Griffith thinks about open source hardware while working with the power-nerds at Squid Labs (*www.squid-labs.com*).

Open Source Electric Vehicle Projects

A preliminary step toward an open source electric vehicle is the solar-powered Vee 9, with downloadable plans available at *www.solarvehicles.org.*

Open source plans for a solar tricycle are available here: *www.uprightsolar.com.*

DORK BOT

Warehouse of wild, weird, and wonderful projects.

By David Pescovitz

Karen Marcelo

Photography by (clockwise from top): Saul Albert, Douglas Repetto, courtesy of Karen Marcelo,
courtesy of Karen Marcelo, Douglas Repetto, Douglas Repetto, courtesy of Karen Marcelo, Douglas Repetto

"I feel like I should watch out for attacking robots, explosions, or giant electrical sparks," said a waiter at a small San Francisco café called Farley's as he approached a group of coffeehouse patrons I was chatting with. It may sound like an odd comment, until you consider the company I was keeping.

I had visited the joint to interview Karen Marcelo, a computer programmer and member of Survival Research Laboratories, the robotic art performance group. Karen runs Dorkbot-SF, a semi-monthly confab where engineers, artists, and designers informally present their work, critique each other's efforts, share technical tips, and drink lots of beer. The motto of Dorkbot-SF, a spin-off of the original Dorkbot-NY, is "people doing strange things with electricity."

"Dorkbot is like informal peer review," Marcelo says. "The work you present doesn't have to be finished. It might even just be an idea that you want feedback on."

By the time Marcelo and I arrived at Farley's, Eric Paulos, another Survival Research Laboratories veteran and machine-art provocateur, was typing away at a scientific paper based on his "urban computing" work at Intel Research. Tesla-coil maestro Greg Leyh, who had just knocked off from his day job designing power converters at the Stanford Linear Accelerator Center, was reminiscing with Paulos about their victory at the recent Power Tool Drag Races, an annual event where "chopped chainsaws and supercharged speed wrenches go head-to-head down 50 feet of drag strip."

Maker

"Dorkbot's raw, unfinished presentation style creates the atmosphere of a personal tour through each participant's workshop, garage, or playspace."

Paulos and Leyh were in attendance when Marcelo held the first Dorkbot-SF meeting in a hacker household during the summer of 2002. I was also at the first Dorkbot-SF — as a presenter. I felt a bit out of place, considering the strangest thing I've done with electricity is create the tangle of extension cords, multi-outlet strips, adapters, and assorted cables behind my desk. But Marcelo had invited me to help launch Dorkbot-SF with a pot-stirring discussion on the sticky relationship between hackers, artists, merry pranksters, and the media.

That night, Brian Normanly really provided the appropriate opening ceremony for Dorkbot-SF. He took the audience outside to gather around the utility pole. Normanly, who resembles an old-time carnival barker, explained the tools and techniques necessary to "liberate and redistribute electricity" — essentially by tapping into the power lines before they reach the utility company's power meters.

Since then, a dozen Dorkbot-SF sessions have been held at various locales, from the Abstrakt Zone live/work loft in post-industrial Oakland, to the minimalist Rx Gallery-cum-sake bar. The events are always standing room only, filled with riot nrrrds eager to listen, learn, and libate. Each evening's program of two or three presenters, selected by Marcelo with input from her co-conspirators, is nothing if not eclectic. Some presentations are polished, many ramble, and a few are incomprehensible train wrecks. But all are interesting.

"Dorkbot's raw, unfinished presentation style creates the atmosphere of a personal tour through each participant's workshop, garage, or playspace," says Paulos, whose Dorkbot talk explored how new wireless technology may dramatically alter our relationships with the "familiar strangers" we encounter every day.

For example, Andrew Bennett showed images from his Absorption Dye Machine that "prints" digital pictures on a massive grid of white carnations. At another meeting, Leyh outlined his dream to build the Advanced Lightning Facility, a pair of 12-story high transformers that spit out 300-foot lightning bolts. Maribeth Back demonstrated an interactive children's storybook — embedded with radio frequency identification (RFID) tags — that she developed at Xerox PARC. And science-fiction author and mathematician Rudy Rucker ranted about cellular automata software and asked the packed house to consider that reality may actually be a highly advanced computer simulation.

The original Dorkbot was founded four years ago in New York City by Douglas Repetto, a computer-music instructor at Columbia University. Repetto had just moved to the city and was searching, he says, for "artists, hackers, engineers, activists, and crackpots hacking away in the back room on some obsession.

"I wanted to create an environment where lots of different sorts of people could come together and share those obsessions," he says. "There's something really compelling about being in the very room where something strange is happening. You're not reading about it, it's not streaming video, it's not a photo slide show. It's right there in front of you. Something might break. And that's good, and invigorating, and exciting."

After Dorkbot-NY was born, the meme spread like lightning. Now there are Dorkbots in more than a dozen cities around the world, from Melbourne to Seattle to Barcelona. When Marcelo first heard of Dorkbot from friends in London, she knew it would be a magnet for San Francisco's tightly-knit population of geeks and gearheads.

"There's an incredibly high density of engineers in this city," says Marcelo. "Even if they can't find work, they're still doing interesting projects on their own. And San Francisco is small enough that collaborations can occur at the spur of the moment."

Dorkbot-SF. Nothing's shocking.

David Pescovitz is co-editor of the popular blog *boingboing.net* and a contributor to Wired and *TheFeature.com*.

Make:Projects

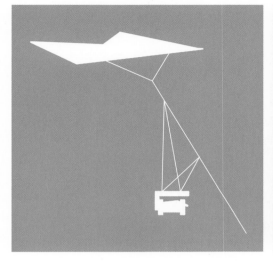

Kite Aerial Photography

50

$14 Video Camera Stabilizer

84

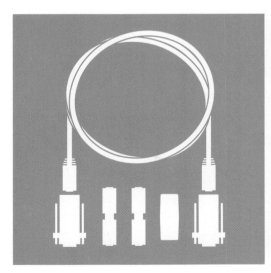

5-in-1 Network Cable

96

Magnetic Stripe Reader

106

"Kite aerial photography appeals to that part of me, perhaps of all of us, that would slip our earthly bonds and see the world from new heights. An aerial view offers a fresh perspective of familiar landscapes, and in doing so challenges our spatial sensibilities, our grasp of relationships."

—Charles C. Benton

Here are four kite aerial photography rigs, all designed and built by Benton. The camera orientation and the shutter buttons of the three rigs on the left are controlled by remote. The rig you'll be making, shown far right, uses a Silly Putty-based timer to activate the shutter once the kite is aloft.

KITE AERIAL PHOTOGRAPHY PUTS YOUR EYE IN THE SKY

By Charles C. Benton

To take pictures from a kite, you need three things: a kite, a camera, and a special rig that attaches the camera to the kiteline and activates the shutter button on the camera. Here's how to do it. >>

Set up: p.60 Make it: p.62   Use it: p.82

HAVE YOU EVER WANTED TO TAKE PICTURES FROM THE SKY?

Kite aerial photography (or KAP for short) bridges the gap between taking pictures from a ladder and taking them from an airplane. Within this elevation spectrum, you can capture landscapes, objects, architecture, and people in entirely new ways.

In the pages that follow, I'll give you step-by-step instructions for building a very low-cost rig consisting of a camera cradle made of craft (popsicle) sticks and model airplane plywood, a shutter-button timer mechanism that uses rubber bands and Silly Putty, and a camera-stabilizing suspension.

Following the step-by-step section, I'll recommend some kites and other equipment you can use for the project, and then run you through your first flight with the rig.

Charles C. Benton *(arch.ced.berkeley.edu/kap/kaptoc.html)* is an inveterate tinkerer from Berkeley, California where he serves as a Professor of Architecture for the University of California, Berkeley. Benton's research in Building Science often involves the design and construction of prototype devices.

KITE AERIAL PHOTOGRAPHY
is a low-cost way to take pictures from heights between 25 and 250 feet.

All you need is a kite, a camera (digital or film), a camera rig consisting of a cradle and a suspension system, and a fairly steady wind. The rigs can range from very simple, single-shot devices (like the one you'll make in this project) to complex affairs with wireless remote viewers, and remote control camera controls. (See sidebar, *Way to Go Pro*.)

Use a high-quality kite with a kiteline rated at a minimum of 100LB test strength to avoid a mishap with a falling camera.

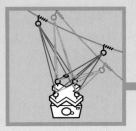

The camera hangs from a Picavet suspension made of kiteline or string, which adjusts for any sudden kite movements.

The double-lever shutter linkage uses two rubber bands: one to provide tension on the Silly Putty timer, and another to push down on the shutter button.

The frame, or "cradle," is used to secure the camera in place and to provide a structure for the shutter lever linkage.

This project calls for a single-use film camera, but the cradle could be modified to work with a digital camera (beware of crash landings if you're a beginner).

Silly Putty inserted in a tube makes for an ideal viscous timer. The rubber band pulls the pin, applying torque to a dowel in the tube. The pin rotates until it frees the rubber band, and ... click!

a b c d

1 min.

Illustration by Nik Schulz/L-Dopa.com

A DAY IN THE LIFE OF A KITE AERIAL PHOTOGRAPHER

It's a sunny Saturday morning in Berkeley, California. I check the Bay Area winds website and learn that a sea breeze is coming from the northwest. My kite aerial photography (KAP) gear is already packed and in the trunk of my VW Cabriolet. The remote control batteries are charged and ready to go. Around noon I head for the Aeroschellville airstrip north of San Francisco Bay. The owner of a Swift airplane wants me to take some photographs of his craft while it is parked on the ground, and he has secured permission from airport authorities to allow me to fly the kite at the airstrip. During the delightful, top-down drive north, I'm watching trees, water surfaces, and so on to get a sense of the wind.

After arriving at the airstrip, it takes less than a minute to clip the fuzzy tail to the kite's harness and to clip the kite's bridle to the kiteline. With a leather glove on the hand I use to hold the kiteline, I launch the kite, a Sutton Flowform 16, and spool out a quick 100 feet of line. Though the kite is behaving somewhat erratically, it has sufficient pull to lift the camera rig. It will be a challenge to avoid motion blur in the images. I would normally send the kite much higher before attaching the camera to see if I can find smoother air at 300 or 400 feet. But this strategy is not prudent at an airstrip, and besides, we would have to seek additional permissions.

It's time to rig the camera, so I clip the kiteline off to a carabiner tied to a post. From my KAP gear bag I pull out a Canon Rebel X, its 24mm lens, and my handbuilt, radio-controlled camera cradle. I spend a minute getting a fresh roll of film into the Canon and the lens-hood mounted on the lens. Then I complete a quick ground check of the remote control radio gear — used to control the orientation and shutter of the camera when it's in the air — by powering up the receiver. Convinced the frequency is clear, I turn on my transmitter and check the camera cradle's rotation functions.

Today's windy conditions invite the inevitable question, "How do you establish a stable platform that you actually trust your camera to?" Even though the kite is quite active a hundred feet up, the movement at the Picavet is modest. This is partly due to the stretch of the Dacron line absorbing the load, but mostly it's just the geometry of having the Picavet within 15 feet of the kiteline's anchor point. When launching, I always attach the Picavet's "hangups" in a position that places the Picavet's cross just within reach — say about 8 feet above the ground. Even if the kite dives 50 feet, the camera will still be above ground level. So I proceed by attaching the camera cradle to the Picavet and making a final check of rig movement functions and the camera's settings: auto-exposure mode, focus on automatic.

Once the camera is hanging from the rig, I unclip the kiteline from the carabiner and gain a little working height by letting out kiteline. As stable as the launching arrangement is, I generally feel better when the camera is clear of the ground. With the camera rig about 30 feet above the ground, I work with the Swift owner to take a series of bird's-eye view and oblique shots of the airplane with the camera gaining no more than 40 feet of altitude

Photography courtesy of Charles C. Benton

(as monitored by the IR laser rangefinder I keep in my vest). The owner helps me sight the camera cradle's position downrange — something my twin sons usually attend to.

The camera cradle is bouncing around quite a bit in the gusty winds and my shutter speed is varying between $1/250$ and $1/500$ of a second (determined when the camera was on the ground). The trick in this situation is to patiently wait for the moments when the camera cradle becomes less active and shoot in these interludes. This I do, and when the rig is moving vigorously, I back away from the handsome Swift, lest something fail, and — bombs away. (I will knock on wood and say that in hundreds of flights, I've yet to drop anything.)

After taking my last shot, I tie the kiteline off to the carabiner again and walk the kiteline down to retrieve the camera rig. With the kiteline under my armpit, I easily handle the Picavet without putting tension on its lines. After removing the camera cradle, the kiteline is released and the kite flies from the carabiner while I move the camera rig out of harm's way (or, as I do on other occasions, change the film and then reattach).

With the camera tucked away, I walk the kiteline down again and remove the Picavet and then the hangups. These go back into their photographer's vest storage pockets. Next the kite is hauled in (by walking the kiteline down in this case) and kite, tail, and kiteline are stowed away. A final scan around the flying site for scattered gear is followed by stowing the larger items, including the photographer's vest, in the KAP gear bag. The session ends by taking a couple of ground-level context shots, thanking the Swift pilot, and exchanging business cards. The total time between hauling out the KAP gear bag and placing it back in the trunk is about 35 minutes.

KAP Around the Globe»

KAP aficionados often emblazon their gear with cloth club badges like the ones shown here.

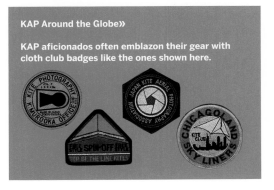

Clockwise from upper right:

Beechcraft 18, Daytona Beach, Florida
(Canon S400 Digital Elph)
When scouting for subjects, I often look for juxtapositions that play well from my low-altitude vantage point. On seeing this derelict Beechcraft 18 mounted on a post above a miniature golf course, I had to stop and shoot. Taking the shot involved flying the rig blindly from the other side of a low-rise hotel.

Point Bonita Lighthouse, Marin County, California
(Canon Rebel SLR w/ 15mm fisheye lens)
Point Bonita guards the northern flank of the Golden Gate Straight. Its lighthouse is perched precariously low on the outermost rocks to keep it underneath the fog. The foundation outline of a former keeper assistant's cottage is visible in the foreground. The barrel distortion of the rectilinear fisheye lens evokes the Earth's curvature.

Pueblo Bonito, Chaco Canyon, New Mexico
(Canon Rebel SLR w/ 24mm lens)
Since my earliest studies in architecture, I have been en-thralled by the great pueblos of the Southwest and speculations about the ancient civilizations that built them. Flying above Pueblo Bonito was a particular treat.

Pigeon Point Lighthouse, San Mateo County, California
(Canon Rebel SLR w/ 24mm lens)
Dense fog marked my drive out to this lighthouse, threatening the inaugural flight of my single-lens, reflex KAP rig. Just as I arrived, the fog, visible in the photograph, pulled back a couple hundred yards and stayed politely out of my way.

Clockwise from upper left:

Children's Play Structure, San Francisco, California
(*Yashica T4*)
Viewed from the ground, this climbing structure appears
as chaotic as the children it entertains. But from the air, its
structure and organization read as clearly as an architectural
blueprint. The exposure was taken under the diffuse light of a
cloudy day, lending a soft quality to the shot. The Yashica T4 is
an impressively capable point-and-shoot camera.

Moored Boats at the Berkeley Marina, Berkeley, California
(*Yashica T4*)
Many subjects reveal a different nature in plan view (looking
straight down), and so it is with boats. One can't help but
wonder about the variety of boat shapes evident in this image
— narrow beam vs. broad, blocky vs. sleek — and the reason-
ing behind each design. Murky water and boat shadows lend
a tangible presence to San Francisco Bay's surface.

The S.S. Jeremiah O'Brien, San Francisco, California
(*Canon Rebel SLR w/ 24mm lens*)
The Jeremiah O'Brien is one of two remaining Liberty Ships,
an anachronistic supply vessel from World War II. It was lov-
ingly restored to operating order by a group of veterans and
enthusiasts. In my early days of kite flying, I once tangled a
kite in the ship's upper rigging. It was extricated by a willing
and able septuagenarian to whom I remain grateful. Practice
with those kites!

SET UP.

MATERIALS:

Braided Dacron fishing line [A]
For Picavet suspension and Ping-Pong ball telltale. 42' L, 80LB test.

1 Brass outer timer tube [B]
Contains Silly Putty and anchors rubber bands. 6" L, ¼" Ø.

4 Pieces vinyl tubing [C]
Used to connect split rings to Picavet arms. ¼" Ø, ¾" L.

1 Finish nail (brad) [D]
Serves as pin for timer mechanism (clip off pointed end). 1" L.

1 Hardwood dowel [E]
Plug for the outer timer tube. 3/16" Ø, 3" L.

3 Hardwood dowels [F]
Pegs to secure rubber bands. 3/16" Ø, 3/8" L.

4 Hardwood dowels [G]
Arms for Picavet cross. ¼" Ø, 5" L.

1 Horseshoe tack [H]
Constrains short shutter lever. 9/16" W.

2 Soft aluminum wires [I]
Used for connection to kiteline. 9/16" Ø, 4" L.

1 Hardwood block [J]
Hub for the Picavet cross. 1¼" L x 1¼" H x ½" thick.

1 Brass inner timer tube [K]
Rotates slowly in outer timer tube filled with Silly Putty. 5/32" Ø, 4" L.

5-ply model aircraft plywood [L]
Backplane for vertical posts and rubber band anchor. 6" L x 1⅞" H x 3/32" thick.

1 Aluminum bracket [M]
Connects cradle to Picavet cross. 8¼" L x ¾" H x ⅛" thick.

2 Hardwood blocks [N]
Serve as left and right posts. 4" L x ¾" H x ½" thick.

1 Ping-Pong ball [O]
Used as a telltale or visual indicator that an exposure has taken place.

1 Craft (popsicle) stick [P]
For shutter nubbin. 1" L x 3/8" H.

1 Craft (popsicle) stick [Q]
For inner part of short shutter lever. 2½" L x 3/8" H.

2 Craft (popsicle) sticks [R]
For outer part of short shutter lever. 3" L x 3/8" H.

1 Craft (popsicle) stick [S]
For inner part of long shutter lever. 3¾" L x 3/8" H.

2 Craft (popsicle) sticks [T]
For outer part of long shutter lever. 4½" L x 3/8" H.

Rubber bands [U]
Power shutter lever and secure camera. #31, 2½" Ø.

6 Split rings [V]
Provide guides for the Picavet suspension lines. 5/8" Ø.

4 Sheet metal screws [W]
Attach backplane to vertical posts. #8, 5/8" L.

1 Metal ring [X]
Constrains center lines of Picavet suspension. 3/8" Ø.

1 Toothpick [Y]
To wedge glass bead on to telltale string.

1 Glass or plastic bead [Z]
Provides a stop on the telltale line. 3/8" Ø.

Silly Putty [AA]
Used in timer.

1 Screw protector [AB]
Finishes end of small timer tube. #6, ½" L.

2 Bolts with lock nuts [AC] [AD]
Join shutter levers and shutter nubbin. 4-40, 5/8" L.

Bolt, washers, and wingnut [AE]
Joins Picavet cross to angle bracket. 8-32, 1" L.

1 Sheet metal screw [AF]
Attaches long shutter lever to right post. #8, ¾" L.

2 Nylon spacers [AG]
Adjust positioning of shutter levers. #8, ⅛" and ¼" L.

1 Nylon bolt and wing nut [AH]
Connects angle bracket to right post. ¼"-20, 1" L.

Craft (popsicle) sticks [AI]
Spares to mix glue or replace a popsicle stick element that splits.

1 Scrap tamping dowel [AJ]
Serves as tamper for inserting Silly Putty. 3/16" Ø, 5" L.

1 Kodak MAX single-use camera

White glue and 5-Minute Epoxy
To attach wooden parts.

1 Kite
See pg. 82 for help in choosing a kite.

TOOLS:
Drill (or drill press), Bits, Hammer, Needle-nose pliers (or large tweezers), Clamping jig, Woodworking vise or bar clamp, Paper clamps (a dozen or so), Wood saw, Miter box, Grinder (or metal cutter and file), Ruler, Phillips-head screwdriver, Pencil, Sandpaper, Piece of scrap wood (for drilling thru-holes), Scissors, Matches (or a lighter), Glue gun

OPTIONAL TOOLS:
Paintbrush

OPTIONAL MATERIALS:
Acrylic paints
Water-based sealer

Key
Ø= diameter
L= length
H= height
W= width

Visit *makezine.com/01/KAP* for source list.

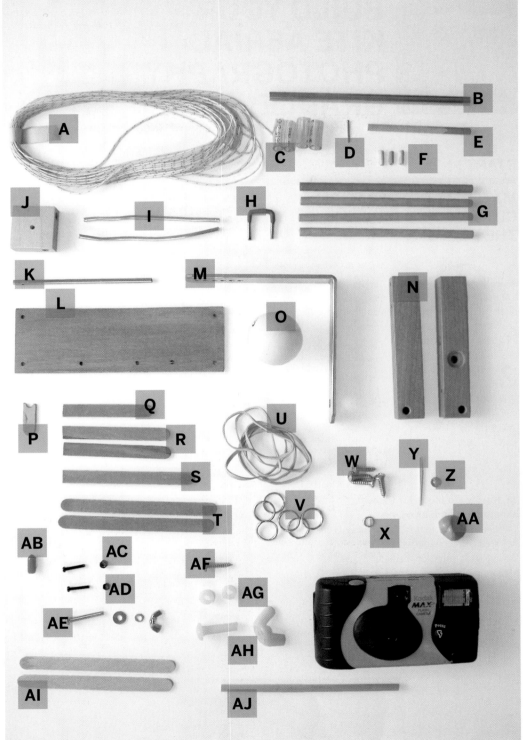

MAKE IT.

BUILD YOUR KITE AERIAL PHOTOGRAPHY CRADLE

START ⠶⠶

MATERIAL PREPARATION: CUTTING AND DRILLING THE PARTS

It's a good idea to cut all the pieces to size and drill all the holes in one session. This will speed up the assembly process.

1. CUTTING

Refer to the list of materials on the *Set Up* page for the dimensions of all parts. The wood pieces can be held and cut with a wood saw and an inexpensive miter box.

If you are making several rigs at once, it makes sense to batch-process them.

2. DRILLING

Tools:

Drill (or better yet, a drill press)

Drill bits: 1/16", 3/32", 7/64", 1/8", 9/64", 1/4", 5/16", 5/32", and 1/2"

Clamping jig

Here are the drilled and cut components for several kits.

2a. Hardwood block for Picavet hanging bolt and arms.

The 1¼" square block of hardwood **[J]** requires a 9/64"-diameter hole drilled through its center for the 8-32 Picavet hanging bolt **[AE]**. You then drill four ¼"-diameter holes in a pinwheel fashion for mounting the Picavet arms **[G]**. The holes should be deep enough to break through the intersecting per-pendicular dowel hole, but note that they should not go completely through the block. I found a small clamping jig very useful in making these dowel holes with the drill press.

9/64" Ø center thru-hole

¼" Ø blind hole (center ¼" from edge as shown)

The hub of the Picavet needs holes for the Picavet dowels and for the hanging bolt. (While I have not tried it, you may be able to substitute a Tinkertoy hub for this part.)

2b. Brass tube for Silly Putty timer mechanism. Mount the vinyl screw-protector cap **[AB]** on the end of the brass ⁵/₃₂"-diameter inner timer tube **[K]** and drill a ¹/₁₆"-diameter hole through the cap and tube, approximately ⁵/₁₆" from the end of the brass tube. This hole is for the clipped 1" finish nail **[D]** that serves as a timer pin. Adjust the hole diameters if necessary.

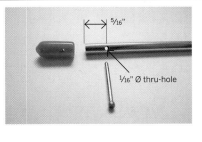

5/16"

1/16" Ø thru-hole

The small hole in the brass timer tube and protector cap will accommodate the timer pin that holds the rubber band.

Clip the pointed end, not the head, of the finish nail.

2c. Plywood for cradle backplane. Drill a ¹/₈"-diameter thru-hole, ¼" in from the edge in each corner of the model aircraft plywood backplane **[L]**. These holes are for the #8 sheet metal screws **[W]** that will mount the backplane to the vertical posts **[N]**. The backplane also receives three asymmetrically spaced ³/₃₂"-diameter thru-holes for the rubber band pegs **[F]**.

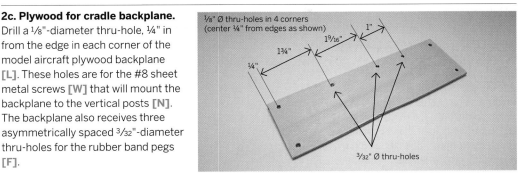

1/8" Ø thru-holes in 4 corners (center 1/4" from edges as shown)

1"

1 9/16"

1 3/4"

1/4"

3/32" Ø thru-holes

2d. Aluminum bracket that connects cradle to Picavet. The aluminum bracket **[M]** is bent from an 8¼" section of ¹/₈"-thick x ³/₄"-wide aluminum bar. Drill a ¼"-diameter hole ⁵/₈" from one end for the ¼"-20 nylon bolt **[AH]** that will attach it to a cradle post **[N]**. At the other end, drill a series of six ⁹/₆₄"-diameter holes for the 8-32 Picavet hanging bolt **[AE]** as shown.

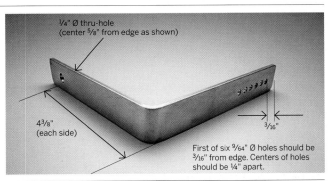

1/4" Ø thru-hole (center 5/8" from edge as shown)

4 3/8" (each side)

3/16"

First of six 9/64" Ø holes should be 3/16" from edge. Centers of holes should be 1/4" apart.

2e. Hardwood blocks that serve as left and right cradle posts. Drill a ¹/₈" hole in the right cradle post for the shutter lever screw **[AF]**. Drill a ¼"-diameter hole through its side for the aluminum bracket **[M]**. The hole needs to be countersunk with a ½"-diameter bit. The upper front of the left post also requires two ⁷/₆₄"-diameter holes for mounting the horseshoe tack **[H]**.

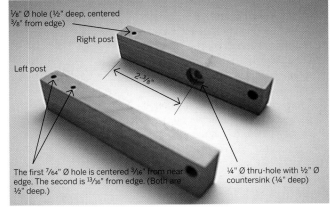

1/8" Ø hole (1/2" deep, centered 3/8" from edge)

Right post

Left post

2-3/8"

The first 7/64" Ø hole is centered 3/16" from near edge. The second is 13/16" from edge. (Both are 1/2" deep.)

1/4" Ø thru-hole with 1/2" Ø countersink (1/4" deep)

2f. Backside of cradle posts. Drill two ⅛"-diameter holes in both posts for the backplane mounting screws **[W]**. Drill ¼"-diameter holes through each post, centered ¼" from the front and the bottom for the brass outer timer tube **[B]**.

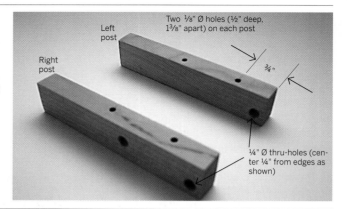

Two ⅛" Ø holes (½" deep, 1⅜" apart) on each post

Left post

Right post

¾"

¼" Ø thru-holes (center ¼" from edges as shown)

2g. Horseshoe tack and timer release pin. One last step in the materials preparation is to remove the sharp points from the horseshoe tack **[H]**, which is used as a pivot for the short shutter lever **[Q] [R]**, and from the finish nail **[D]**, used as a release pin for the inner timer tube **[K]**. I did this with a grinder, but diagonal metal cutters and a file would work as well.

The horseshoe tack and finish nail should have their sharp points removed. I found a supply of these electrical cable tacks that come with a nice blue, plastic coating – how elegant.

Note: Some additional drilling will be necessary in Step 7: Adding the Shutter Levers.

NEXT ››

ASSEMBLY DIRECTIONS

Now that all the parts have been cut to size and drilled, you can begin assembly. You'll be flying a camera in no time.

3. PREPARATION

Materials (optional): Acrylic paints, water-based sealer
Tools (optional): Paintbrush

3a. Gather all components. Start by finding a nice clean surface (I use an inexpensive sheet of poster board) and lay out the materials. Identify each item using the photo in the *Set Up* section as a guide, and verify that your kit is complete.

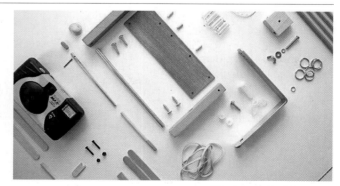

It is always a good idea to review the entire instruction set and kit components before starting a project.

3b. Decide whether you will apply a finish to the wooden components of the rig. If you intend to do so, now is a good time. I think the rig looks great with a bit of color. I use water-diluted acrylic paints to stain the kit's wood components. Once the stain is dry, I seal it with a coat or two of water-based sealer. I used Liquitex acrylic paint, diluted one part paint to two parts water, followed by water-based Varathane.

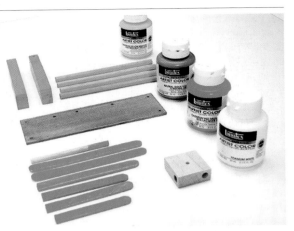

All of the kit's wooden parts are candidates for paint. The craft sticks, dowels, and posts shown here are already painted.

4. GLUING

Materials: White glue or 5-Minute Epoxy, craft sticks (for mixing epoxy), four or so paper clamps
Tools: Hammer, needle-nose pliers (or large tweezers)

The next step is gathering the components that require gluing. While many joints in the kit are candidates for glue, there are four for which it is mandatory: 1) adding pegs **[F]** to the cradle backplane **[L]**, 2) installing the plug **[E]** in the outer timer tube **[B]**, 3) assembling the long shutter lever **[S] [T]**, and 4) assembling the short shutter lever **[Q] [R]**.

It is often sufficient to "press fit" the remaining joints (join them without glue), but if any union seems loose, a little glue may be in order. While wood-on-wood joints work well with conventional white glue (Elmer's), this type of glue takes a while to set. If you are in a hurry or are building the cradle in a single session, then a two-part epoxy (5-Minute Epoxy) works well. Installing the plug **[E]** in the outer timer tube **[B]** requires a thicker glue and 5-Minute Epoxy works well here. The following instructions assume you are using 5-Minute Epoxy and should allow you to glue all joints from a single batch of mixed epoxy.

4a. Plug outer timer tube. Plug one end of the outer timer tube **[B]** with the 3" hardwood dowel **[E]**. The plug will be a loose fit in the outer timer tube and will require thick glue to secure it.

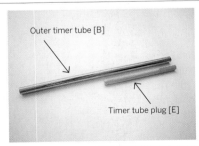

Outer timer tube [B]

Timer tube plug [E]

The timer tube plug will be glued inside the outer timer tube. Silly Putty will fill the remaining space in the tube.

4b. Prepare long shutter lever.

Position the parts for the long shutter lever [S] [T] as shown, with the shorter craft stick [S] in the middle. Place a mark ¾" in from the rounded end of the inner stick [S] to ensure accurate placement of the other sticks when gluing.

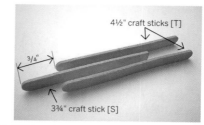

4½" craft sticks [T]

¾"

3¾" craft stick [S]

When gluing these sticks, you want to make sure that glue is spread evenly on both sides of the inner stick.

4c. Repeat for the short shutter lever.

This lever uses craft sticks [Q] and [R]. These are aligned differently than those in the long shutter lever. In this case, just align the rounded ends of the sticks with the shorter stick in the middle.

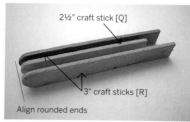

2½" craft stick [Q]

3" craft sticks [R]

Align rounded ends

Note the different alignment for the short shutter level.

4d. Set up pegs and backplane.

Position the plywood backplane [L] on a sheet of paper. Place the three short segments of ³⁄₁₆"-diameter dowel [F] as shown in this rear view.

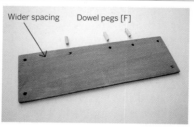

Wider spacing   Dowel pegs [F]

The three middle holes will hold small pegs for anchoring rubber bands.

4e. Mix epoxy.

Follow instructions on the glue tube. You'll be placing the two glue components on a disposable mixing surface and mixing them thoroughly with a spare craft stick.

Use a scrap of cardboard and a spare craft stick to mix the 5-Minute Epoxy.

4f. Seal plug.

After the glue is mixed, apply a liberal amount to the plug [E] for the outer timer tube [B] and push the plug inside the tube. The dowel's end should be roughly flush with the tube's end. Wipe off excess glue and set the assembly aside to cure.

Plug in place

The plug has now sealed off the end of the outer timer tube. This allows us to use less Silly Putty later.

4g. Glue levers. Apply glue to both sides of the inner stick of the long shutter lever **[S]**, then position the outer sticks **[T]** (remembering to leave ¾" of the inner stick exposed). Clamp with paper clamps and wipe off excess glue. Repeat the process with the short shutter-lever components.

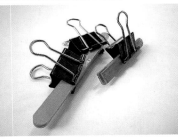

The 5-Minute Epoxy cures quickly, so we will be able to proceed without much of a delay.

4h. Glue pegs. One-by-one, dip the short pegs **[F]** in the glue and place them in the asymmetrical holes in the backplane **[L]**. I position them with a pair of needle-nose pliers. A light tap with a hammer is usually sufficient to press them into the holes. Make sure that they are flush with the front side of the backplane.

I use a pair of needle-nose pliers to hold the pegs in position while I tap them in place with a hammer.

4i. Inspect work. Here's the finished product, showing the pegs projecting out from the rear of the backplane. The pegs are flush with the front side of the backplane. The remaining holes (two on each side) are for mounting the backplane on the vertical posts.

"We'll See About That"

A MAKER STORY

Burrell Smith was a 23-year-old, self-taught engineer, hired into Apple in February 1979 as Apple employee #282, a lowly service technician responsible for fixing broken Apple IIs.

Bill Atkinson was the main programmer for the Apple II Pascal system. He was in the service department picking up some extra language cards when Burrell heard him lamenting about overflowing the Apple II's memory limitations.

"Well, why don't you add more memory to the language card?" Burrell suggested.

Bill was intrigued, but he complained. "You can't add any more memory because we're out of address space."

"Well, the language card is already bank-switching the RAM, even double-banking the last 2K where the monitor ROM is. We'll just make it bank-switch another bank." Burrell built him a prototype. It worked like a charm, and soon Burrell was busy manufacturing 80K language cards for all the Lisa programmers.

Around this time, Bill ran into Jef Raskin. Jef had been writing a series of papers about a consumer-oriented computer that would be extremely inexpensive and radically easy to use. Bill introduced Burrell to Jef, saying, "Jef, this is Burrell. He's the guy who's going to design your Macintosh for you."

"We'll see about that," Jef replied. "We'll see about that."

– Andy Herzfeld (via folklore.org)

Excerpted from Revolution in The Valley. Copyright© 2004 Andy Herzfeld.

5. A PRESSING ENGAGEMENT

■ **Materials:** White glue **Tools:** Woodworking vise or bar clamp, ruler

Now that the mandatory gluing is complete, we can make the next round of connections. The joints in these sections can be made in two different ways: they can be glued or they can be "press fit" if the match between the opening and the component is tight enough. So try the joints described in this section for a preliminary fit. If the pieces fit snugly, a press fit is probably sufficient. If they are loose, then use glue. (If the connections in step **5b** are loose, hold off on the glue until step **6b**.)

We will begin the press-fit process by first connecting the brass outer timer tube **[B]** to the two vertical posts **[N]** (pay attention to the orientation of the tube's plugged end), and we'll finish with assembling the cross for the Picavet suspension by joining the Picavet cross arms **[G]** to the Picavet hub **[J]**.

Both vertical posts **[N]** have a ¼"-diameter lateral hole through the bottom front to hold the brass outer timer tube **[B]**. Unlike the left-hand post, the right-hand post (as seen from the front of the rig) has a hole sideways through its center for the bracket mounting bolts. Unlike the right-hand post, the left-hand post has two small holes through the top front for mounting the horseshoe tack **[H]**. Take some time to get these posts oriented correctly and life will be blissful.

5a. Position posts and tube. This view shows the vertical posts from the back side as indicated by the two upward-facing, predrilled holes for mounting the backplane on each post. Note that holes for the brass outer timer tube are located near the table's surface. Note also that the right post (seen on the left because we are viewing from behind) is oriented so that the large side of the middle hole is facing inward.

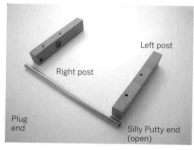

Left post

Right post

Plug end

Silly Putty end (open)

Make sure the plug end of the outer timer tube is oriented toward the right post (the post with the large hole in the middle).

5b. Press tube into posts. I used my woodworking vise to press the brass outer tube into its corresponding openings in the vertical posts. Check orientations of the components before pressing. The fit between tube and opening in some kits may be a bit loose. In this case you will not require a vise but may require a little epoxy. Mount the backplane (see next section) before using the epoxy.

Lack access to a woodworking vise? A short bar clamp can provide the same function. Make sure the components are lined up well before applying the pressure.

5c. Position parts that form the Picavet cross. Arrange the hardwood center hub **[J]** and the four hardwood dowel arms **[G]**, lining them up with the holes they'll be pressed into.

Make sure that drilling debris is cleared from the arm holes before the arms are inserted. I use a small nail to clear out shavings.

5d. Insert dowels into hub. As each arm is inserted, note that it will eventually rest against the inserted arm adjacent to it. For instance, the end of dowel A in the photograph will rest against the side of dowel B after insertion. Similarly, the end of dowel B will rest against the side of dowel C. Therefore, do not press a dowel completely in until its adjacent dowel is at least partially in place.

Dowel C
Dowel B
Dowel A

A closer view of the center hub. The ¼" dowel arms fit into the holes in a pinwheel fashion.

5e. Press-fit dowels into hub. Again I used my woodworking vise to press the Picavet arms into their holes in the center hub. The fit was sufficiently tight that I could not have done this by hand. Glue was not required.

If your dowels slide in more easily, just place them by hand and then secure them with a little wood glue.

Each Picavet arm should project from the center hub approximately 4¼ inches. Check with a ruler and adjust as necessary.

5f. Alternative. A bar clamp offers an alternate means for pressing the arms into place. As with the woodworking vise, line your parts up straight and gently press them together.

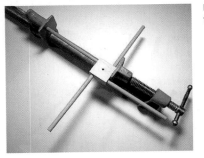

Bar clamps are commonly found in wood shops.

5g. Place the Picavet cross aside temporarily. We will finish fitting it out later. The Picavet cross should be light and strong.

Remember, if your parts do not fit snugly, add a bit of white glue to tighten things up, and allow it to cure overnight. Or use Epoxy if you're moving quickly.

6.
ADDING COMPONENTS TO THE CRADLE
■ **Materials:** Epoxy **Tools:** Phillips-head screwdriver

Now that the glue for the backplane pegs has cured, we can start assembling the camera cradle itself. These steps should go pretty quickly. As in the previous sequence, take care that the vertical posts and backplane are oriented correctly. The backplane should have pegs projecting from the top rear of the rig, and these pegs appear to be a bit more toward the right-hand side when viewed from the rear.

6a. Place the backplane [L] over the two vertical posts (now joined by the brass outer timer tube [B]). Align the backplane's predrilled holes with their complements in the vertical posts. Note that you may have to work the posts a little closer together or further apart to align the holes. Find the four #8 sheet metal screws [W] that join the backplane to the posts.

The backplane is screwed to the back of the vertical posts without glue. Note that the pegs for the rubber bands are facing away from the posts. This properly places them at the rear of the cradle.

6b. Secure backplane to vertical posts with screws.

If the brass tube was a loose fit in step **5b**, now is the time to secure it with a bit of glue (before screwing the backplane to the posts).

6c. Position small cradle parts.
Locate the horseshoe tack [H], aluminum bracket [M], and ¼"-20 nylon bolt and wing nut [AH]. Place them in position relative to the cradle.

These small parts will be mounted on the cradle.

6d. Place bracket on cradle. Align the aluminum bracket with the mounting hole in the cradle's right-hand post, and push the nylon bolt through the post and the bracket with its threads pointing outward.

The nylon bolt head should fit nicely into its ½"-diameter countersink.

6e. Secure bracket on cradle with wing nut. Just attach the nylon wing nut and the bracket is secured to the cradle. How's that for a short step?

The wing nut will allow you to quickly adjust the camera's tilt relative to the horizon before sending it up for a shot.

6f. Press the horseshoe tack [H] into place. Use the two holes predrilled in the front face of the left-hand post. Ideally, the tack will have a snug friction fit with the holes. I have found it convenient to remove this part on occasion, so if you use glue, use it sparingly.

The horseshoe tack constrains and guides the shutter-lever system.

6g. Finished sub-assembly. This sequence should have taken you all of three minutes. The next step is a little more challenging: configuring and mounting the double-shutter lever system.

Here is the cradle at the end of this stage. It's starting to look like something useful.

7. ADDING THE SHUTTER LEVERS

Tools: Drill press or hand drill, pencil, needle-nose pliers, sandpaper, screwdriver

Now it is time to assemble and mount our shutter-release system, beginning with the levers. When we last encountered these pieces (in step **4g**), they were just a few craft sticks glued together. They are now about to become a nicely articulated, compound-lever shutter-release system. This step will involve a bit of minor drilling.

7a. Drill mounting hole in long shutter lever.
Find the long shutter lever and identify the end that has the middle craft stick projecting ¾" from the two that sandwich it. Drill a hole at this end of the lever with a ⅛"-diameter bit. This will be the mounting hole for the pivot end of the lever.

Craft sticks are a bit prone to splitting when drilled, so take these drilling steps nice and slow.

7b. Assemble levers.
Now find the short shutter lever and nest its "gapped" end within the similar end of the long shutter lever. You will need to leave a small gap, as shown in the figure, to allow clearance for the hinge to move. Mark the position of the hinge line with pencil.

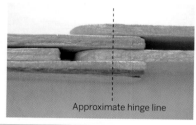

Approximate hinge line

This view shows the two lever assemblies from the bottom.

7c. Drill hinge-pin and rubber band hole.
Drill a ⁷⁄₆₄"-diameter hole for the 4-40 bolt that serves as a hinge pin **[AC]**. While we are drilling, change to a ⁵⁄₃₂"-diameter bit and make a hole at the outer end of the short shutter lever. This will hold the rubber band that connects that lever to the Silly Putty timer.

Use a block of scrap wood when drilling thru-holes.

7d. Collect lever hardware.
Now, rummage through the parts bag and find the ⅝"-long 4-40 bolt **[AC]**, which serves as the hinge, and its lock nut. While you are looking, also find the ¾" sheet metal screw **[AF]** and ⅛" nylon spacer **[AG]** that will be used to mount the pivot end of the long shutter lever.

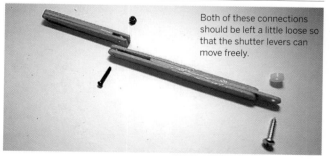

Both of these connections should be left a little loose so that the shutter levers can move freely.

7e. Hinge shutter-lever arms together with 4-40 bolt.
Use needle-nose pliers (or any nut immobilizer of your choice) and a screwdriver. Slip the assembled shutter levers through the horseshoe tack on the left vertical post.

Since we want these parts to move back and forth around the hinge, make sure you do not tighten the assembly too much. This is why we are using a lock nut.

7f. Attach lever to cradle post.
Secure the pivot end to the right post using the #8 sheet metal screw **[AF]**. The 1/8" nylon spacer goes between the lever and the vertical post. We want this connection to move as well, so do not over-tighten. Do not allow the long shutter lever to project past the outer edge of the right post as this will interfere with the angle bracket. This is a trial fitting. You will remove the levers later to mount the shutter nubbin **[P]**.

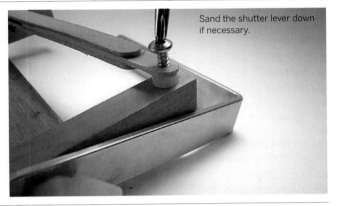

Sand the shutter lever down if necessary.

8. INSTALLING THE INNER TIMER TUBE
Tools: Glue gun

The next steps are pretty easy. We will assemble the inner-tube portion of the timer mechanism, stuff the outer timer tube with Silly Putty, and squish the two together.

8a. Collect timer hardware.
Locate and align the inner timer tube **[K]**, the plastic cap (screw protector) **[AB]**, and the clipped 1" finish nail **[D]**. While you are at it, grab the Silly Putty **[AA]** and tamping dowel **[AJ]**, too.

The holes are drilled approximately 5/16" from the end of the tube.

8b. Place cap on tube.
The inner timer tube **[K]** and the plastic cap **[AB]** have holes that align when the cap is placed on the tube. Once the holes are aligned you can install the finish nail **[D]** through the hole (going in either direction). I put a quick squirt of hot glue inside the end of the inner timer tube with the drilled hole as insurance against the pin falling out.

Note that the end of the finish nail has been clipped off.

8c. Stuff outer timer tube with Silly Putty. Find the little blob of Silly Putty **[AA]** and the short length of $^3/_{16}$" dowel **[AJ]** to use as a tamper. Roll a bit of Silly Putty into a line and drop it into the outer timer tube. Repeat until the tube appears full. Then use the dowel as a tamper to press the Silly Putty deeper into the tube. Add more Silly Putty and tamp into place. Repeat until the timer half of the tube is full.

You will notice later that the Silly Putty leaks out of the outer timer tube over time. Don't fret. It took a full year before I needed to add more Silly Putty to replace the leakage.

8d. Insert inner timer tube into the Silly Putty that fills the outer timer tube. This will go slowly, perhaps taking a couple of minutes, so be patient. Just apply modest, consistent pressure and the inner timer tube will slide all the way in until it is stopped by the outer timer tube's plug **[E]**. It does not matter which direction the inner timer tube's finish nail is facing.

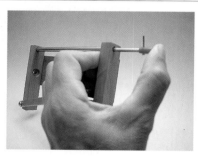

This really is a step you should take slowly. The Silly Putty's viscous nature that makes this slow is the same property that makes the timer work.

9. MOUNTING THE CAMERA AND ADJUSTING THE TIMER COMPONENTS

■ **Materials:** Epoxy **Tools:** Drill, pencil, pliers, screwdriver

Now that the timer is assembled, we can set about making a few minor adjustments to fit the cradle to the camera. The instructions for the shutter-lever assembly up to this point have assumed we are using a Kodak MAX single-use camera. It is pretty easy, however, to adapt the cradle to other camera geometries.

9a. Attach rubber bands to timer tube. Start by taking a couple of #31 rubber bands **[U]** and hitching them to the brass outer timer tube as shown in the image. Just run the rubber band around the tube and then back through itself.

The outer timer tube serves as structure, camera support, hitching rail, and timer mechanism.

9b. Attach camera to cradle. Take your camera and fasten it to the cradle using the two rubber bands. I allow the bands to cross over each other as they go over the camera, and then secure them to the pegs at the top of the backplane.

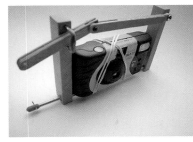

You might notice at this stage that the Silly Putty has rebounded a bit. Just rub off the excess and push the inner timer tube back in. It will stabilize after a few such iterations.

I keep a couple of empty cameras on hand for setting up the cradles. Processing labs will generally give you a couple of used ones for free.

9c. Adjust shutter lever location. Examine the relationship between the camera's shutter button and the long shutter lever. If the center gap of the long shutter lever is centered over the shutter button, you are in good shape. If an adjustment is required, you can shift this center gap by changing the size of the nylon spacer **[AG]** or mounting the shutter nubbin **[P]** on one of the outer faces of the shutter lever.

This step determines the location of the shutter nubbin relative to the front and back of the camera.

9d. Position shutter nubbin. Find the shutter nubbin **[P]**, made from a craft stick remnant, and place it in the center gap of the long shutter lever. Adjust its position to the left or right of the cradle until it's over the center of the camera's shutter button. Mark the nubbin's position on the long shutter lever and the long shutter lever's position on the nubbin with a pencil.

Note that you can also adjust the position of the camera slightly to the left or the right of the cradle to aid in aligning the shutter nubbin.

9e. Attach shutter nubbin to lever.

Once the shutter nubbin location is established, remove the shutter-lever assembly from the cradle and drill a 7/64"-diameter hole for the 4-40 bolt **[AD]** that secures the shutter nubbin to the lever arms. Use your pencil-mark guides to make sure the two parts are correctly aligned. Install the bolt, tighten it enough to secure the shutter nubbin, and remount the shutter-lever assembly on the cradle.

If you prefer, you can glue the shutter nubbin in place rather than bolt it. Use a clamp until the glue sets.

9f. Install a third #31 rubber band on the outer timer tube "hitching rail" and remount the camera.

Route this compression band past the front of the camera, over the shutter nubbin, and secure it on a backplane peg. Install a fourth #31 rubber band on the end of the short shutter lever. Just poke it through the 5/32"-diameter hole and loop it through itself. This tension band will connect to the Silly Putty timer.

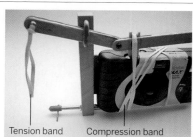

Tension band   Compression band

The tension rubber band powers the Silly Putty timer and serves as a release linkage. The compression rubber band drives the shutter release nubbin into the shutter button once the tension rubber band is released.

9g. It is time to test your Silly Putty timer. (Insert sound of drum roll here.) Follow these steps:

i) Place a test camera in the cradle.

ii) Turn the release pin on the inner timer tube to a position level with the ground or slightly downward.

iii) Pull the short shutter lever downward and slip the tension/linkage rubber band over the timer tube pin.

iv) Make sure the shutter nubbin is now raised clear of the shutter button.

v) Cock the camera by advancing its thumbwheel film advance.

vi) Wait patiently while the timer release pin rotates slowly to face upward. This can take a long time when the Silly Putty is freshly installed.

vii) When the shutter fires, you can dance the jig of joy and hug your neighbors. Ta da!

The initial tuning of your timer is largely an exercise in balance. You can adjust forces in the system. For instance, stretching a rubber band a few times will loosen it and lessen its driving force. Putting an extra turn of rubber band at a connection point will effectively shorten it and increase its driving force. Make adjustments of this sort until the short shutter lever causes the shutter nubbin to hover just above the shutter button when the system is cocked. When the tension band slips the timer pin, the compression band should have ample force to fire the shutter.

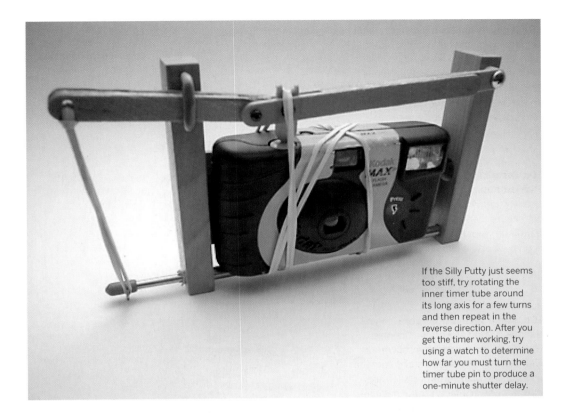

If the Silly Putty just seems too stiff, try rotating the inner timer tube around its long axis for a few turns and then repeat in the reverse direction. After you get the timer working, try using a watch to determine how far you must turn the timer tube pin to produce a one-minute shutter delay.

10. COMPLETING THE PICAVET SUSPENSION

Tools: Matches or lighter, scissors, pliers

The rig is almost complete. Now we need to work on the Picavet cross that we pressed/glued together in step **5**. This involves attaching a metal ring to each end of the cross, making two kiteline hangers for our connection to the kiteline, and finally, threading the Picavet suspension line back and forth to connect the cross to the hangers.

10a. Attach rings to Picavet. Find the six ⅝"-diameter metal rings **[V]**, the short sections of ¼" vinyl tube **[C]**, and the length of Dacron line **[A]**. Cut four 8"-long and one 24"-long lengths of line from your braided Dacron stock **[A]**. Attach each 8" length of line to its own metal ring using a Lark's Head knot. Now, attach a ring to the end of each Picavet arm by running the tails of the Lark's Head through the vinyl tube and then sliding the tube over the end of the dowel.

The friction fit of the vinyl tube holds the metal ring in place nicely.

Lark's Head Knot

10b. Secure the Lark's Head tails.
Knot them on the top of the Picavet arm, crossing the tails over one another, and knotting again on the bottom of the arm. After the knot is secure, you can trim the excess tails and singe the line ends to prevent fraying.

The ring should be snug with the arm, but with enough play to rotate 90 degrees or so.

10c. Install Picavet hardware to the Picavet hub [J]. Assemble the 8-32 bolt, washer, and wing nut **[AE]**, which will secure the Picavet to the cradle's aluminum bracket **[M]**. The wing nut is on the bottom side of the cross.

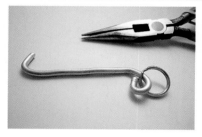

This wing nut is used to (pre)aim the camera in different directions.

10d. Make Picavet hangers. Take the two 4"-long pieces of aluminum wire **[I]** and bend them as shown with a pair of pliers. One end is turned upward a bit while the other is formed into a downward-facing loop that captures the remaining metal rings **[V]**.

When the kiteline is wrapped four or five turns around the wire, even slight tension on the kiteline will hold the wire firmly in place.

10e. Add suspension lines to the Picavet. Take the remaining 24" of the braided Dacron line **[A]** and thread it through the metal rings on the cross and kite attachment clips. The threading sequence is:

A1 - 1 - B1 - R - 4 - A2 - R - 2 - B2 - 3 - A1

The letters **A** and **B** refer to the attachment clips, the numbers **1** through **4** the ends of the cross, and the letter **R** a small 3/8"-diameter metal ring **[X]** used to constrain the center lines of the Picavet where they cross.

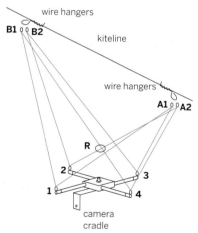

wire hangers

B1 B2

kiteline

wire hangers

A1 A2

R

2   3
1   4

camera
cradle

To thread the suspension line, I just place the cross and kiteline attachments on a clean surface and work the line through the sequence. When the threading is complete, tie the tail end of the line to the front end (a Sheet Bend knot works well).

Sheet Bend Knot

10f. Tie up suspension lines. As you will undoubtedly discover, the Picavet suspension lines are prone to tangle when the cross is not hanging from the kite. When storing and moving the Picavet, it is wise to daisy-chain the Picavet lines together. The suspension lines unzip from this series of loops quickly when deploying the rig.

While hard to explain, the Daisy Chain knot is easy to tie. Here is a photo of the suspension lines while I was tying a daisy chain.

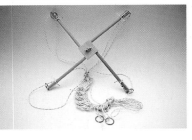

An image of the completed Picavet with its suspension lines daisy chained.

After completing the chain you can cinch (tighten) the last loop to lock the chain in place.

10g. Mount the aluminum support bracket [M] in place on the right side of the cradle. Use a finger to balance the cradle so the camera tilts neither to the left nor the right. The hole above your finger in the upper surface of the support bracket is the one you should use for mounting the Picavet cross using the bolt and wing nut [AE].

Balancing the camera cradle in this fashion makes it less likely that the horizon will be tilted in your photographs.

11. CONSTRUCTING AND ADDING EXPOSURE TELLTALE
Tools: Drill

The final construction step is assembling and connecting the "advanced Ping-Pong ball exposure-event indication system," or exposure telltale. When the tension band is released, the telltale is dropped, letting you know the shot has been taken.

11a. Assemble telltale components. Find the Ping-Pong ball [O], glass or plastic bead [Z], and toothpick [Y]. These are combined with a 24"-length of Dacron line to make the telltale.

11b. Drill a ⅛" hole through the Ping-Pong ball. Thread the Dacron line through this hole and tie a knot that prevents it from slipping back through. Slip the glass or plastic bead on the line and position it 2" or so from the Ping-Pong ball. Wedge the bead in place with the toothpick and snap off the excess length of the toothpick.

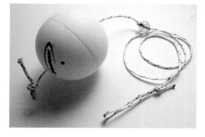

Attach the telltale system by tying it to the inner timer tube where it projects from the left-hand post.

11c. Compare your rig to the photograph above. When completed, the entire rig should look like this.

Congratulations. It's now time to take your project on a test flight!

FINISH ☒

NOW GO USE IT »

SAFETY CONSIDERATIONS

For a more complete list of safety precautions, please visit my website at *arch.ced.berkeley.edu/kap/background/safety.html.*

Wear gloves. I always wear a leather glove to protect my kiteline-holding hand. (I am right-handed, so it is a right-hand glove.) In three years, I have been through about 10 gloves. Watching the abuse they take and their eventual modes of failure provides compelling evidence to continue the practice.

Supervise kids. Be careful not to let a child fly a large kite without supervision. Kids often want to pull on the kiteline; I let them do this only while I hold onto the reel.

Develop knowledge of the local winds and weather. In the San Francisco Bay Area, we have wind patterns that vary with topography, season, and time of day. Often the wind builds up toward a small-craft warning in the summer afternoons. If you have a large kite up when the wind builds in, then getting it down can be unintuitively dramatic (voice of experience here). Spend some time observing winds at your KAP site. Ask folks who have developed experience at the site. If you are unfamiliar with a setting, then be cautious. You might consider flying a small kite for a while just to get a feel for the winds.

In the Bay Area, we have a stable atmosphere and few cumulous clouds. Lightning is rare for us, but not so elsewhere. If electrical storms occur where you fly, avoid kite flying during their presence. Don't push your luck with atmospheric electricity; we know better today.

Protect yourself from the sun. One of the nicer aspects of flying kites is the time spent outdoors. Be prudent with the sun, however, as it can cause serious injury and lead to disease in the skin and eyes. Protective clothing, sunscreen, sunglasses, and moderation are in order.

Have the means to anchor the kite. If the wind does fill in, it is useful to have a means of securing the kiteline to an anchor (e.g., lamp-post, tree, fence, bench, car). I carry a climber's strap and carabiner for this purpose. Slip the strap around the anchor and the kiteline on the carabiner with a clove hitch, and the inanimate anchor is under stress, not you.

Practice small before flying large. I started with small kites and gained hundreds of hours of practice before flying large kites. It is much easier to learn the vagaries of a kite and the wind with a 16-square-foot kite and 100-pound line than with their larger brethren.

Avoid flying near people and property. In general, do not fly where a kite mishap could cause injury to people or damage to vehicles and ground structures. The most straightforward way to avoid striking people or things is not to fly near them. Most of my early KAP outings were to rural or seashore settings where I had consistent wind and plenty of room. At times, your kite and rig will seem stable. Experience will help you judge whether to trust this apparent stability.

Take care with your mounting details. It is probably self evident that you have a lot riding on your mounting connections. Make certain that these connections are trustworthy before using them above people and property. The connector of the KAP cradle to the Picavet cross is a good example, as is the Picavet line itself. Failure of either will cause the dreaded "bombs away" scenario. Some KAPers run a safety tether between camera and kiteline.

Know your kite. Develop some experience with a kite before using it to lift cameras. My Sutton Flowform can collapse and drop under low velocity and turbulent conditions. When my Rokkaku thermals, it sometimes wants to invert (to my dismay) and fly itself into the ground. Learn the vagaries of your own kites and watch them for odd behavior. Check your bridles periodically as well. If a crash is inevitable, it sometimes helps to let the kiteline go slack before impact. Keep an eye on your gear for wear and tear.

Have room to back up. Select a flying site that allows you enough room to back out of trouble. If the wind fails momentarily, running upwind can create enough "breeze" to fly the kite and lift the rig, thus carrying you through the moment. I always want a clear area behind me when photographing people, and I say as much to folks hanging around me. At least once a month, I find myself dropping the transmitter and backing up (often while hauling in line) to keep the KAP rig in the air.

Be aware of airport locations. The FAA restricts kites weighing more than five pounds from flying within a five-mile radius of any airport. While lighter kites are exempt from this requirement, it is prudent to know the location of nearby airports and to avoid flying in areas that align with their runways. This information is readily available on a map; look it up before you fly. I have flown my kites at small airports before, but only after receiving permission from the airport manager. Note that airplanes often neatly align with the runway as they approach to land, but their departures follow varied paths.

USE IT.

CHOOSING A KITE AND SENDING UP THE RIG

With the rig complete, you are undoubtedly giddy in anticipation of a first flight. Here are some tips to make the most of it.

CHOOSING A KITE

Most KAP photographs are taken using single-line kites, and there is an entertaining world of possibilities for you to choose from. There is much to appreciate in the steady lift of a workhorse kite, and like so much else in modern life, finding the ideal kite takes a bit of care. I recommend starting with a soft kite — that is, a kite that doesn't have rigid struts. I've grown very fond of my soft kites, and if the wind allows, they are my first choice. They establish and hold their shape with air pressure, and lacking rigid spars, they are easy to set up and take down. They do like a steady breeze. The Sutton Flowform #16, which costs about $95, is a solid workhorse kite, and can be purchased from *kapshop.com*. For a detailed discussion about kites, see my page at *arch.ced.berkeley.edu/kap/equip/equip.html*.

SENDING UP THE RIG

It is best to begin in an open, uncrowded setting with a steady breeze; a beach or large park works well. If you have not read the *Safety Considerations* section, do so before going out. Don't forget to take, and use, a glove for handling the kiteline. Look upwind before you launch the kite. The landscape should be open in this direction to avoid turbulence and to give you room for maneuvering should the wind lapse. After rigging and launching the kite, you should spool line out until the kite flies smoothly. This distance is usually 100 feet or so, but can vary with terrain and wind conditions. At this point, I just fly the kite for a while with the goal of understanding the site's wind patterns. Are the winds steady or variable, strong or weak?

a. Attach rig to kite. If the winds are favorable, it is time to mount the Picavet suspension and camera cradle. Tether the kiteline to a friend or other anchor. Then attach the two aluminum wire hangers (**10d**) on the kiteline about five feet apart by wrapping the kiteline five or so times around the wire. Tension will then hold the attachments in place. Mount your camera in the camera cradle and attach the cradle's aluminum bracket to the center hub of the Picavet cross. Check the camera cradle for balance — if it is leaning to one side or the other, you can shift the mounting holes.

Ground-level view of the camera rig flying below a Sutton Flowform 16 kite. The Picavet suspension lines are white in this image. The camera cradle is well balanced below the Picavet cross.

b. Set the Silly Putty timer, camera shutter, and Ping-Pong ball telltale. (Remember to set the timer before cocking the camera.) We are getting close now. Think about the composition of your first shot and adjust the camera cradle's direction and tilt using the wing nuts. Check to see if the camera is level with the horizon. If not, just adjust the position of the Picavet cross.

With timer set and shutter cocked, the camera rig is sent skyward, by letting out kiteline.

c. Spool out more kiteline and watch your camera fly. Once the desired camera height is achieved, you can walk the camera around a bit to fine-tune its position. It is now time for patience as you wait for the Ping-Pong ball to drop. Three minutes can be an incredibly long time!

When the Ping-Pong ball drops, the timer has fired and your photograph is taken.

Once the camera is in position, you wait for the Ping-Pong ball to drop. You then retrieve the camera and repeat to your heart's desire.

d. Reshoot. Rather than pulling the kiteline in, you can walk the line down until you reach the camera. It can then be aimed again, the timer reset, and the shutter cocked for the next shot. Just let the line go when you're finished, and the camera will head skyward again. Once you get the hang of it, this goes quite quickly. If you use this technique, you should be cautious not to interfere with a pedestrian or bicyclist.

Way to Go Pro

Most of my experience in KAP has been accrued with radio-controlled camera rigs carrying 35mm single-lens reflex cameras. A radio link (using an RC transmitter) allows the photographer to aim the camera and control the exact instant of photographic exposure. Furthermore, using a camera with motorized film-advance allows an entire roll of film to be taken without landing the camera. These capacities come with a price tag in the hundreds of dollars and add complexity to the venture.

1. Video transmitter scavenged from a wireless X10 webcam.

2. Picavet suspension made from old hard-disk-drive actuator arms.

3. Model airplane remote-control receiver and servo.

4. Plan rotation gears adapted from RC car parts.

$14 VIDEO CAMERA STABILIZER

By Johnny Lee

You don't have $10,000 to spend on a Steadicam? Make this ultra-low-cost video camera stabilizer and see how much better your video shots turn out. >>

Set up: p.88　**Make it: p.90**　**Use it: p.94**

WHY I BUILT A CHEAP VIDEO CAMERA STABILIZER

Professional camera stabilizers use a complex, levered arrangement to capture smooth-looking video, even when the camera and camera operator are in motion. The camera operator may walk (or even jog), move through tight hallways and doorways, and climb up and down stairs without shaking the camera.

Unfortunately, professional Steadicams cost upwards of $10,000. Even cheap, third-party stabilizers cost at least $600. So I decided to make my own. It cost me $14. Here's how you do it.* Whether you're an aspiring filmmaker, a videographer, the family documentarian, or if you just want more utility out of your video camera, you'll appreciate this video-cam stabilizer.

*Or you can simply buy one from me at *johnnylee.net.*

Johnny Lee (*johnnylee.net*) graduated from the University of Virginia with an engineering degree and an interest in film as a hobby. He ran the student film organization, taught classes in digital filmmaking, assisted in film festivals, and has won several regional awards for his own short films. He is now in graduate school at Carnegie Mellon University pursuing a doctoral degree in Human-Computer Interaction.

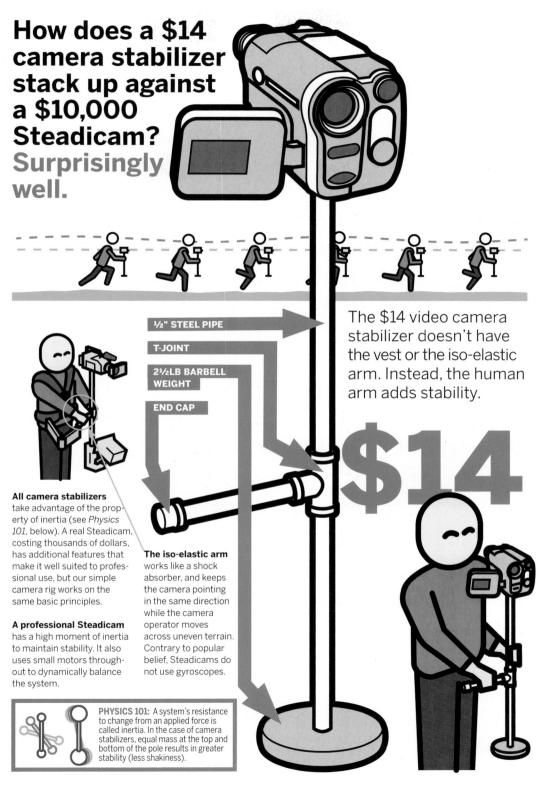

How does a $14 camera stabilizer stack up against a $10,000 Steadicam? Surprisingly well.

½" STEEL PIPE

T-JOINT

2½LB BARBELL WEIGHT

END CAP

The $14 video camera stabilizer doesn't have the vest or the iso-elastic arm. Instead, the human arm adds stability.

$14

All camera stabilizers take advantage of the property of inertia (see *Physics 101*, below). A real Steadicam, costing thousands of dollars, has additional features that make it well suited to professional use, but our simple camera rig works on the same basic principles.

A professional Steadicam has a high moment of inertia to maintain stability. It also uses small motors throughout to dynamically balance the system.

The iso-elastic arm works like a shock absorber, and keeps the camera pointing in the same direction while the camera operator moves across uneven terrain. Contrary to popular belief, Steadicams do not use gyroscopes.

PHYSICS 101: A system's resistance to change from an applied force is called inertia. In the case of camera stabilizers, equal mass at the top and bottom of the pole results in greater stability (less shakiness).

Illustrations by Nik Schulz

SET UP.

Visit *makezine.com/01/stabilizer* for source list.

TOOLS

¼" Drill bit: Must go through galvanized steel. Don't try this with a cheap wood bit; you'll ruin it.

Electric drill.

Pliers.

Screwdriver: The type depends on the bolts you get.

Hammer.

Stationary vise: It's possible to do it without the vise, but it's far more difficult and potentially dangerous.

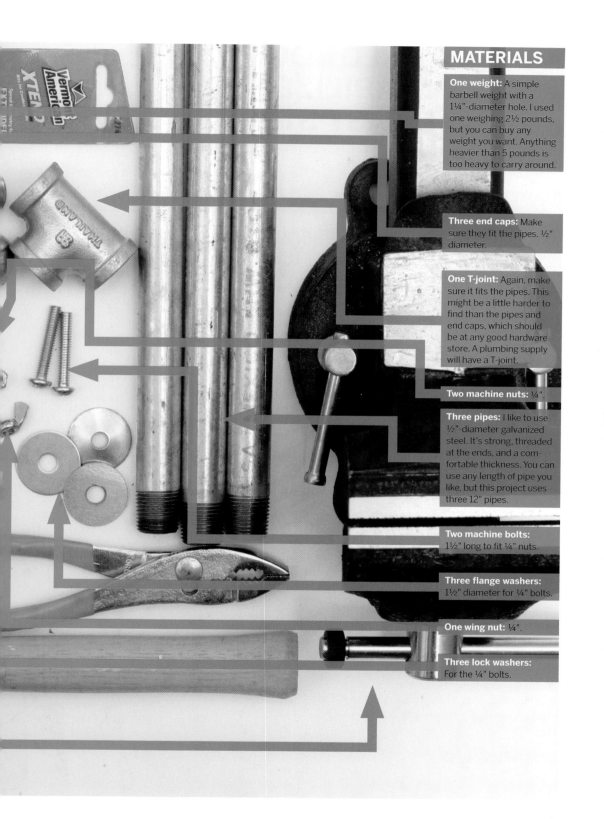

One weight: A simple barbell weight with a 1¼"-diameter hole. I used one weighing 2½ pounds, but you can buy any weight you want. Anything heavier than 5 pounds is too heavy to carry around.

Three end caps: Make sure they fit the pipes. ½" diameter.

One T-joint: Again, make sure it fits the pipes. This might be a little harder to find than the pipes and end caps, which should be at any good hardware store. A plumbing supply will have a T-joint.

Two machine nuts: ¼".

Three pipes: I like to use ½"-diameter galvanized steel. It's strong, threaded at the ends, and a comfortable thickness. You can use any length of pipe you like, but this project uses three 12" pipes.

Two machine bolts: 1½" long to fit ¼" nuts.

Three flange washers: 1½" diameter for ¼" bolts.

One wing nut: ¼".

Three lock washers: For the ¼" bolts.

MAKE IT.

BUILD YOUR STABILIZER IN 5 EASY STEPS

START ⟫

Time: **45 min.** Complexity: **Low**

1. **MAKE THE HANDLE.** This first step is pretty easy. Just attach the T-joint and one end cap to one of the pipes to form a basic handle.

Use the vise for final tightening. Don't use your hands to tighten the T-joint and end cap on the pipe. You'll just hurt yourself and not get it tight enough.

2. **DRILL HOLES IN THE END CAPS.** Put one of the end caps in the vise as shown. Then drill a ¼" hole in the center of the cap. It doesn't have to be perfectly centered, but the closer the better. You really want to use the vise because you're drilling through a quarter inch of galvanized steel. It's enough to bring weak drills to a dead stop and will definitely do a number on your hand if you just try to hold it. Not to mention it can get hot. Protective eyewear such as safety goggles should ALWAYS be worn when using any power tool. Also, a little bit of machine oil (or even vegetable oil) can make this easier and help preserve your drill bit.

Do your drilling in an area that's easy to clean up. You'll produce lots of metal shards. And don't use you fingers to wipe away the shards! They'll get in your skin. Use a brush or a vacuum.

I like using a slow speed because when the bit comes out the other side, it'll jerk from grabbing onto the metal. It's far more pleasant to have a slow jerk than to have the drill suddenly fly out of your hand.

Do this for two end caps.

Photography by Evan McNary

3. ASSEMBLE THE MOUNTING.

The mounting requires a bolt, two lock washers, a flange washer, a nut, the wing nut, and a drilled end cap. Put a lock washer on the bolt and then put it through the end cap. You need to have the bottom of the bolt coming out the top of the outside part of the end cap, as shown here. Put another lock washer on and then the nut. Put the end cap in the vise and tighten the nut with pliers. The lock washers will keep the bolt from turning.

You'll want to make this really tight because this is where your camera attaches. You want it tight not because the camera could fall off, but because putting the camera on and taking it off requires lots of turning action. If this mounting loosens, the bolt will pivot around, as will your camera, making it hard to keep still. If this happens while you're filming, you'll have to stop and find the pliers.

Use a hammer to dent the center of the flange washer. You can do this by putting the washer over the hole in the weight, putting the head of a bolt on the hole, and hammering the bolt. The washer will distribute the force away from the single point of contact. The wider the washer the better. If you don't use the washer, the camera will shake a lot right at this connection, as well as put a great deal of stress on this one tiny spot. It could damage your camera, so if you lose this washer, don't use the stabilizer.

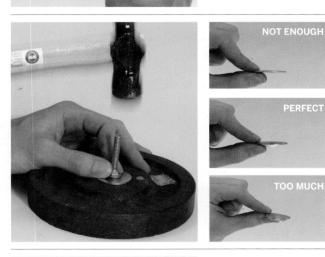

Use your fingers to tighten the wing nut on the mounting. DO NOT use the pliers. You could strip the threads on your camera or break the tripod mount. Both are bad.

4. ASSEMBLE THE BASE.

You'll need the barbell weight and a lock washer, two flange washers, a bolt, a nut, and a drilled end cap. They'll go together in the pattern shown to the right. The bolt goes through two washers that sandwich the weight. Then stick on the end cap, put on the lock washer, and finally the nut. Hand-tighten the parts until they are snug.

The lock washer deep inside the end cap will keep a grip on the nut, so you don't have to stick pliers down there to turn it. Just turn the cap. Then stick the cap in the vise, and use the screwdriver to tighten the bolt, or just grab the weight and turn it. The weight should turn the bolt, and the vise will keep the cap from turning.

I like to tighten the bolt until the outer washer starts to bend inward. This reduces the amount the bolt sticks out, which makes the base more stable when you set it down.

If you use the base as a stand (not recommended because it's easy to knock over), you can buy rounded bolts and little rubber feet. These will make a much nicer base that won't wobble. You can tell I like to do this and I say it's easy to knock over from experience. My camera still works, though.

5. ALL TOGETHER NOW ...

Lastly, take the remaining two pipes, screw them into the T-joint of the handle, and attach the base and the mounting. And you're done! You can tighten these parts as much as you'd like. Either give them a good hand-tightening or the full-fledged vise-and-pliers tightening. The only reason not to use the vise and pliers is if you want to be able to collapse the stabilizer or swap components. You can vary the pipe lengths and barbell weight however you like.

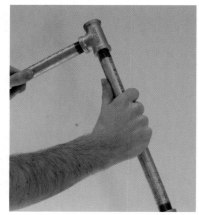

I would probably refer to this combination as the "sport model," mostly because its balance point (with camera) is near the T-joint and can be spun around by the handle pretty well. It's really agile. Longer bars and heavier weights change the handling. (See *Alternative Weights and Pipe Lengths*, page 95.)

When you store your stabilizer without the camera attached, the mounting washer is left unsecured on the end. I recommend taking off the wing nut, putting on the washer, and then screwing the wing nut back on. That will keep the washer from getting lost.

FINISH X

NOW GO USE IT »

A MAKE STAFFER'S EXPERIENCE

A mechanically minded friend and I spent about 45 minutes building this camera stabilizer in my modestly equipped garage workshop. It was generally easy, and we didn't get hung up anywhere.

The hardest part was drilling the holes in the end caps. We used a stationary drill press instead of a handheld drill, which helped considerably. Unfortunately, we didn't do a very good job of centering the drill bit within the end cap. The hole was straight, but it wasn't close enough to the middle for my liking.

Our second drilling attempt fared better because we center-punched the end cap to know where to drill. **One thing, though — you've got to add oil to the end cap as you drill to keep the drill bit from getting dull from the heat.** Luckily, you only need two end caps with holes. If you mess up on one, you can use it as the bottom cap, and try again.

End caps are bulged on top. We flattened them with a file. We could have avoided this step and it would have been fine, but we figured a flat top would make the camera more stable.

We came up with a different way to bend the flange washers. **Our method involved bolting two washers together through the center of the weight like a sandwich (the weight in the middle and the washers on either side, held together by a bolt).** We put this contraption in a vise and used a vise grip to tighten the nut on the bolt until we'd bent the flange washers adequately. The downside of this was that both flange washers ended up bent instead of just the one that we needed. Not the end of the world, but if you're concerned about having a flat flange washer for the bottom piece, pick up an extra one at the store.

I used a 5LB weight and tested it using the video feature on my Olympus D550 camera (which weighs under one pound). The counterbalance was much too heavy for my camera so there was a lot of camera movement in the video. Still, it was better than if I'd been running with just the camera. I plan to buy a lighter weight the next time I pass a sporting goods store so I can give the stabilizer a real workout.

—*Robin Outis*

USE IT.

READY. AIM.
SHOOT STEADY.

THE SIDE HANDLE is used to stabilize side-to-side rocking. (Vertical shaking is pretty much dampened by the weight.) You may hold the handle however you'd like. The way I like to hold it is shown here. How you do it accounts for 80 percent of the smoothness. This is true even with professional equipment with fancy shocks and hydraulics. Don't expect this thing to perform miracles. You have to practice using your arms and body to create a smooth motion. Watch your hands while you walk, and see how level you can keep them relative to the ground. Keep your legs bent and learn how to "glide." I talked with someone who has used a professional camera stabilizer and he said this was "really just as good." Getting good results is not so much about the equipment, but how you use it. That's really true about everything.

Photograph courtesy of Johnny Lee

MODIFICATIONS AND ADD-ONS

The easily unscrewable camera stabilizer lends itself to a number of useful and simple adaptations and enhancements

INVERTING BRACKET

The bad thing about the stabilizer by itself is that it makes it very hard to get ground-level shots (running along the ground while looking up at a person). So, you can build a little inverting bracket that wraps around the camera and allows it to be attached to the stabilizer on the top rather than the bottom. Just flip the whole stabilizer upside down so the weight is now on the top and the camera is on the bottom.

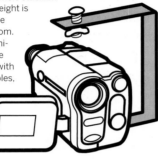

You can buy an aluminum bar at a hardware shop, cut it to length with a hacksaw, drill the holes, and bend it using the vise. Make sure the top hole is exactly above the bottom hole or it will be off balance. Use a ruler to make measurements. You'll lose about ⅛" in the bend, so be careful to account for that. It's also much easier to get a controlled bend if you make a little notch with the hacksaw on the inside where each bend should be.

ALTERNATIVE WEIGHTS AND PIPE LENGTHS

You could use a 24"-long pipe at the bottom and a 5LB weight. This combination produces smoother shots for vertically oriented movement. Tilting the camera is much harder because of the heavier weight and longer arm. So if you want more agility, use the sport version with all 12" bars and the 2½LB weight. Having a variety of lengths and weights is a reason you may not want to tighten everything with pliers. Good hand-tightening is usually enough to keep everything together for a day's worth of shooting. The 24" version is pretty tall. Using the inverting bracket, you can get nice, ground-level running video.

Sport model
12" bars
2½LB weight

Bigger model
24" bottom bar
5LB weight

LARGE SLED PLATFORM

Here's a simple way to add a big platform to the top of the stabilizer for use with larger cameras (or simply so you can turn the mounting nut rather than the camera).

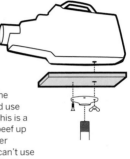

Cut a rectangular piece of wood at least as wide as the base of your camera. Buy a ½" flange to replace the mounting cap on top. Put screws through 3 of the 4 holes of the flange and into the wood platform. Drill a ¼" hole all the way through the platform where the fourth hole in the flange is and use that for your mounting bolt. This is a quick and easy way to really beef up the camera support for bigger cameras. Unfortunately, you can't use the inverting bracket in combination with this platform.

Modification Mailbag

A surprisingly large number of amateur physicists and certified mechanical engineers write fairly long emails pointing out problems with this design and offering suggestions. Here's a small sample:

Suggestion: The bottom weight should be exactly the same weight as the camera (see *Physics 101*, page 87).

Reply: Every camera weight is different. Scales with ounce or gram precision are not common, making it difficult for people to weigh their cameras. Also, weights sold in exact ounces or grams are not easy to come by. If you have access to these, that's great! More power to ya. But 2½LB or 5LB barbell weights from a sports store are close enough approximations for most people with consumer-grade cameras. Unsteadiness produced by disparate weights can also be reasonably overcome with practice.

Suggestion: PVC or aluminum bars would be better than steel.

Reply: You are free to use whatever material you choose, but I like steel piping because it is strong and comes pre-threaded — no cutting, no gluing, no welding. I can collapse the camera stabilizer for storage and reassemble it in less than 30 seconds without using any tools.

Five cables, bad.

One cable, good.

THE 5-IN-1 NETWORK CABLE

By Michael Ossmann

Nothing's worse for a network administrator than being without a needed cable. So I made a single cable to replace the five I used to carry. The result: no more tangles and no more scrounging for a missing link. >>

Set up: p.100 Make it: p.102 Use it: p.105

WHY I MADE A 5-IN-1 CABLE

Do you find yourself toting several of these cables everywhere you go? Do you often wish you'd brought a different cable with you after you've arrived onsite? Are you as geeky as me and think that the idea of a 5-in-1 is just plain cool even if you never expect to configure a router in your lifetime? Then I'll show you how I made one.

The 5-in-1 cable consists of a CAT5 Ethernet cable along with four simple custom adapters, giving me an Ethernet cable, a crossover Ethernet cable, a modem cable, a null modem cable, and a Cisco console cable. An added benefit is that I can always extend my cable by finding a longer Ethernet cable than the one I carry in my bag. (It's usually pretty easy to locate a long Ethernet cable, but not so easy to locate a long null modem cable.)

Michael Ossmann (*ossmann.com/mike*) is a Senior Security Engineer for Alternative Technology in Colorado. He can't think of a second sentence that doesn't sound pompous or stupid.

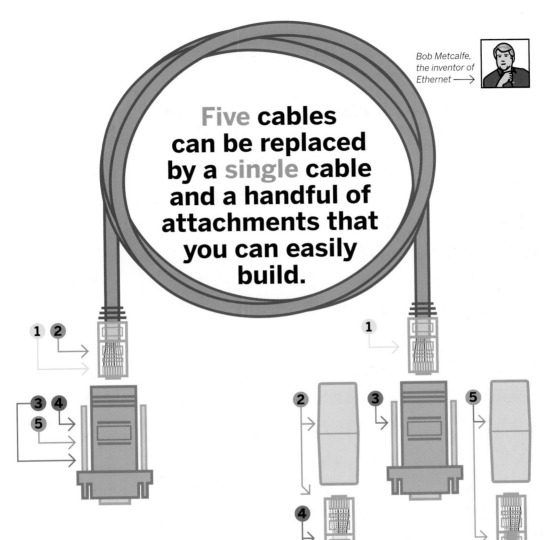

Bob Metcalfe,
the inventor of
Ethernet →

Five cables can be replaced by a single cable and a handful of attachments that you can easily build.

1 Ethernet cable: Ethernet is the standard way to connect computers that are relatively close to each other. Modern CAT5 Ethernet cables carry data over twisted pairs of wires in order to reduce interference, enabling longer cables and faster data rates.

2 Crossover cable: Connecting computers over Ethernet requires a hub or switch to connect the "send" wire on one machine's Ethernet cable to the "receive" wire on another machine's cable. With just two computers, you can ditch the hub and use a crossover cable. Its send and receive wires cross over from one end to the other.

3 Modem cable: A straight-through RS232 serial cable is called a modem cable because it is used to connect Data Communications Equipment (DCE), such as a modem, to Data Terminal Equipment (DTE), such as a dumb terminal or computer. DTE devices are pinned differently than DCE devices so that they can be connected with a straight-through cable.

4 Null modem: The null modem cable is to a modem cable what the crossover cable is to the Ethernet cable. It allows direct serial communication between two nearby devices such as two computers or two modems.

5 Cisco console: This cable is used on certain kinds of Cisco equipment. It is an RS232 null modem cable with a 9-pin plug on one end and an RJ45 plug on the other.

Illustration by Nik Schulz

SET UP.

Visit *makezine.com/01/5in1cable* for source list.

TOOLS

Wire strippers.

Needle-nose pliers to crimp the DB9 pins.

RJ45 crimpers.

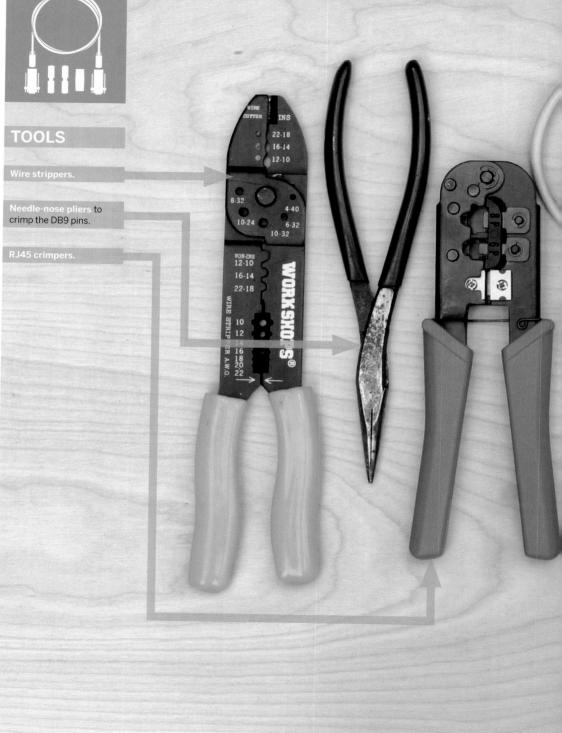

Two short lengths of CAT5 cable, preferably of different colors, about 2 inches long . You can cut up existing Ethernet cables.

Four RJ45 modular plugs. Have extras on hand just in case.

Eight female pins for the DB9 connectors. Have a few extra pins on hand unless you are much more dexterous than me.

Two DB9 female to RJ45 female modular adapters. These are the kind of adapters that let you configure your own pinouts.

One RJ45 coupler. The coupler must have all eight conductors. Be aware that many Ethernet couplers only have four.

One straight-through Ethernet cable. This must be an eight-conductor cable, not a four-conductor cable.

MAKE IT.

BUILD YOUR 5-IN-1 CABLE

START >>

Time: 30 min. Complexity: Low

1. MAKE "THE WORLD'S SHORTEST CROSSOVER CABLE"

You can actually make the crossover cable as long as you want, but the longer you make it, the more you have to carry around.

This cable must cross the pairs that are not used by Ethernet in addition to the pairs that are. This is why you must perform this critical step and cannot use a standard crossover cable you may already own.

1a. Crimp one of the RJ45 plugs on each end. Order the wires on one end according to the following 568B standard (with the clip facing down):

12345678

pin 1: white/orange
pin 2: orange
pin 3: white/green
pin 4: blue
pin 5: white/blue
pin 6: green
pin 7: white/brown
pin 8: brown

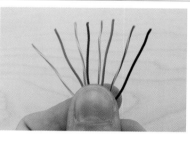

This is the most common order for Ethernet cables, so you could get a head start by snipping off the end of an existing cable; then you only have to do the other end.

1b. Order the wires on the other end this way:

12345678

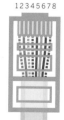

pin 1: white/green
pin 2: green
pin 3: white/orange
pin 4: white/brown
pin 5: brown
pin 6: orange
pin 7: blue
pin 8: white/blue

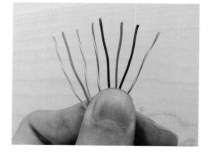

Make sure each pair has at least one twist. Then you can prove people wrong if they scoff, "That's not the world's shortest crossover cable; that's just an adapter!"

2. MAKE THE CISCO CONSOLE ADAPTER

This adapter works with the RJ45 serial port found on most Cisco routers. It also works on some Sun servers. It is important to note that this is not a symmetric adapter. The 568B end will point away from the router and the other end will be inserted into the router. I marked one end with a Sharpie so I wouldn't forget which end was which.

Cisco's (otherwise very helpful) cabling page (*cisco.com/warp/public/701/14.html*) has RTS and CTS reversed on the DB9/RJ45 console cable. I verified this by inspecting an actual Cisco cable. They don't really care because their console ports do not use flow control, but doing it the right way enables interoperability with Sun servers and perhaps some other things.

This is like the crossover cable but with a different pinout.

2a. Make the first end according to 568B again (clip facing down):

```
12345678
```

pin 1: white/orange
pin 2: orange
pin 3: white/green
pin 4: blue
pin 5: white/blue
pin 6: green
pin 7: white/brown
pin 8: brown

You can read about the 568B standard at *www.utm. edu/~leeb/568/568.htm*.

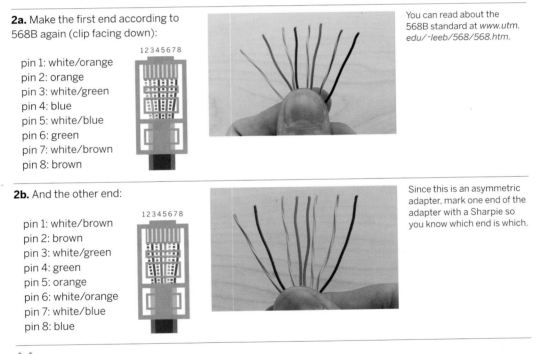

2b. And the other end:

```
12345678
```

pin 1: white/brown
pin 2: brown
pin 3: white/green
pin 4: green
pin 5: orange
pin 6: white/orange
pin 7: white/blue
pin 8: blue

Since this is an asymmetric adapter, mark one end of the adapter with a Sharpie so you know which end is which.

3. MAKE TWO DB9/RJ45 ADAPTERS

This is the trickiest part. In order to make your cable compatible with the largest number of serial devices possible, you need to combine a couple of pins and split another one. Both of the DB9/RJ45 adapters should be wired exactly the same way, regardless of whether they will be used for DTE or DCE devices. Here is the pinout:

DB9 pin	signal	RJ45 pin	color *
1	DCD	8	white
2	RxD	3	black
3	TxD	1	blue
4	DTR	5	green
5	SG	2 & 6	orange and yellow
6	DSR	8	white
7	RTS	4	red
8	CTS	7	brown
9	R		none

* My DB9F/RJ45F modular adapters are colored blue, orange, black, red, green, yellow, brown, white (RJ45 1-8). If yours are different, ignore the colors in the above pinout.

3a. DB9 pins 2, 3, 4, 7, and 8 are easy. Just push the appropriate pin in the back of the DB9 connector until it snaps.

Be careful not to get any of the pins mixed up because errors are a bit difficult to fix unless you have the right tool to pop the pins back out again. Pin extractors are available at *svc.com/mole extractor.html*.

3b. DB9 pin 5 needs two wires connected to it. Snip the pins off of the wires coming from RJ45 pins 2 and 6 (orange and yellow on mine), strip about 3mm off the end of each, and crimp them together onto one of your spare pins.

Use a spare pin to crimp the wires together.

3c. RJ45 pin 8 has to connect to both 1 and 6 on the DB9 connector. Snip the pin off of the white wire, strip the end, cut about an inch of scrap CAT5 and pull out two of the white wires, strip both ends off of them, crimp a pin on each one, and splice all three loose ends together.

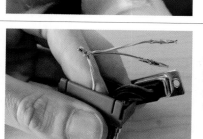

You can break the end off of a spare pin and use it to crimp the three wires together. You can use the other two white wires from the inch of CAT5 for the second adapter.

When you are finished, your Ethernet cable will be pinned like so:

1	TxD	pair one
2	SG	pair one
3	RxD	pair two
4	RTS	pair three
5	DTR	pair three
6	SG	pair two
7	CTS	pair four
8	DSR/DCD	pair four

FINISH X

NOW GO USE IT »

PUTTING YOUR 5-IN-1 CABLE TO WORK

THE FIVE DIFFERENT SETUPS

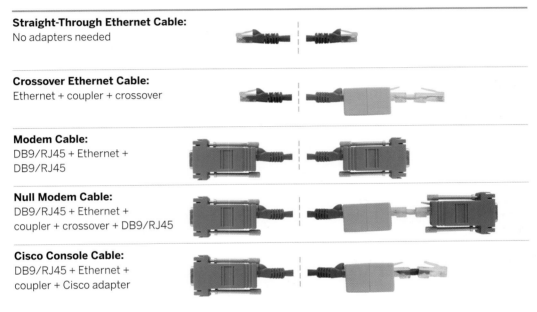

Straight-Through Ethernet Cable:
No adapters needed

Crossover Ethernet Cable:
Ethernet + coupler + crossover

Modem Cable:
DB9/RJ45 + Ethernet +
DB9/RJ45

Null Modem Cable:
DB9/RJ45 + Ethernet +
coupler + crossover + DB9/RJ45

Cisco Console Cable:
DB9/RJ45 + Ethernet +
coupler + Cisco adapter

Remember that the Cisco adapter is not reversible.

NEED A DIFFERENT PINOUT?

If you need a DB9/RJ45 serial cable with different pinouts than the Cisco one, all you have to do is make another little CAT5 adapter. Cable ends are cheap and plentiful.

FAKING FLOW CONTROL

When used as a serial cable, this is a hardware flow control (CTS/RTS) cable. If you are using devices that both require hardware flow control, it should work. If neither of your devices requires hardware flow control, it should still work. However, if one of your devices requires hardware flow control and the other does not support hardware flow control, then you need a cable that fakes flow control. This could be done with an additional DB9/RJ45 adapter or with another CAT5 adapter and some creative crimping (my preference), both of which are left as exercises for the reader.

EXTRA ADAPTERS

Many additional adapters could easily be added to this set. A few that leap to mind would be for other kinds of serial ports such as DB25 and various DIN and miniDIN ports for Macintoshes and other things. For the pinouts for these adapters, please visit my website: *www.ossmann.com/5-in-1.html*.

CHECK YOUR CONDUCTORS

If you grab a random Ethernet cable to use with your serial adapters, remember to make sure that it has all eight conductors. Also keep in mind that most Ethernet cables have only been tested for connectivity on four conductors (1, 2, 3, and 6) if they have been tested at all. I used those conductors for the most important serial signals (Transmit, Receive, and Ground) just in case, but some serial devices won't talk without all eight working.

MAGNETIC STRIPE READER

By Billy Hoffman

Have you ever wondered what information is stored on the magnetic-striped cards in your wallet? Now you can find out. This project shows you how to make a magstripe reader for less than $40. »

Set up: p.109 Make it: p.110 Use it: p.117

WHAT'S ON YOUR CREDIT CARDS?

Open your wallet. How many cards in there have magstripes on them? If you're like me, the answer is five or six. Ever wonder what's encoded on them?

I did. One day a friend of mine had a $200 off-the-shelf magstripe reader, so I ran my cards through it. Aside from the expected credit card numbers, I was surprised by the amount of personal information encoded on them. In fact, for reasons I still don't know, two cards contained my Social Security number.

Magstripes are everywhere in the developed world, but aside from a few academic papers and hacking articles, very little information is published about them. So I looked into it and ended up designing my own magstripe reader, interface, and software. This project shows you how I did it, and how you can, too.

Billy Hoffman is a computer science major at Georgia Tech, who has written and lectured about privacy and security. He is the creator and lead developer of Stripe Snoop. You can email him at Acidus@msblabs.org.

HOW THE MAGSTRIPE SYSTEM WORKS

To find out what's on your cards, you need three things: (1) an inexpensive magstripe reader to read the data stored on your cards (which you'll modify to work with your PC's game port), (2) a parallel port adapter (you won't need this if your PC has a game port — see *Making a Parallel Port Adapter*, p.113) and (3) the Stripe Snoop open source software (download from *stripesnoop.sf.net*).

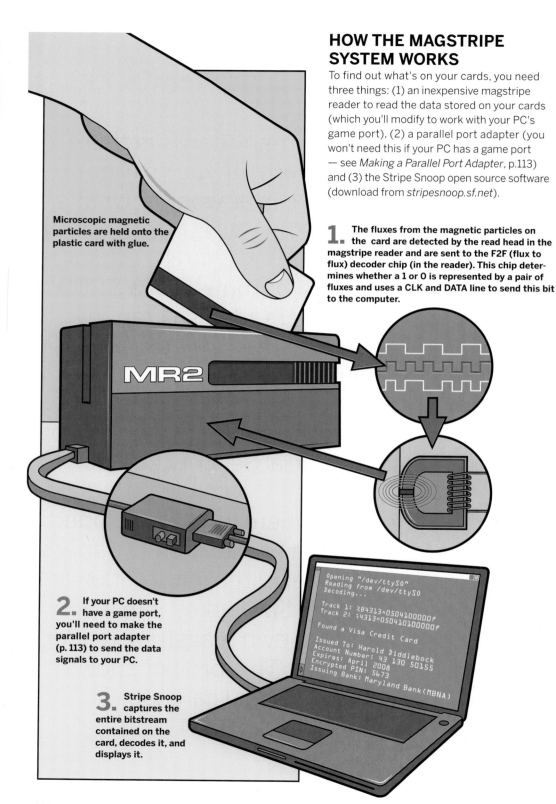

Microscopic magnetic particles are held onto the plastic card with glue.

1. The fluxes from the magnetic particles on the card are detected by the read head in the magstripe reader and are sent to the F2F (flux to flux) decoder chip (in the reader). This chip determines whether a 1 or 0 is represented by a pair of fluxes and uses a CLK and DATA line to send this bit to the computer.

2. If your PC doesn't have a game port, you'll need to make the parallel port adapter (p. 113) to send the data signals to your PC.

3. Stripe Snoop captures the entire bitstream contained on the card, decodes it, and displays it.

```
Opening "/dev/ttyS0"
Reading from /dev/ttyS0
Decoding...

Track 1: %B4313^05041000000?
Track 2: ;4313=05041010000000?

Found a Visa Credit Card

Issued To: Harold Diddlebock
Account Number: 43 130 50155
Expires: April 2008
Encrypted PIN: 5673
Issuing Bank: Maryland Bank (MBNA)
```

Illustration by Timmy Kucynda

SET UP.

Visit *makezine.com/01/magstripe* for source list.

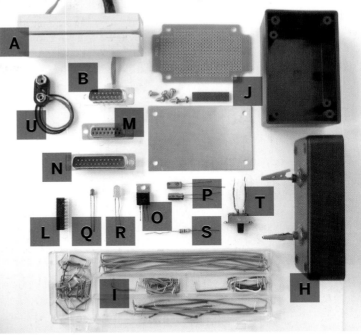

TOOLS AND MATERIALS

Card reader

TTL Magstripe reader [A] I recommend the Omron V3A family, specifically the V3A-4, which you can purchase online from Digikey (www.digikey.com). TTL readers aren't very hard to find: you can get one for less than $5 from BGMicro (www. bgmicro.com).

DB-15 Male connector [B] This is a joystick connector. Make sure you don't get a DB-15HD, which is a VGA connector. You won't find these in your local RadioShack so you'll need to order part #15034 online at www. jameco.com.

Cat 5 cable [C] You'll need about 4 or 5 feet. You can buy this by the foot from Home Depot or Lowe's, or just scavenge it from an unused Ethernet cable. (Speaker cable could also be used, but you will need an additional 8 to 10 feet of it.)

Soldering iron and solder [D] Any light duty soldering iron and solder will work. I got mine years ago at RadioShack.

Electrical tape [E] This will protect our soldering and make the finished product look better.

Hot glue gun [F] A glue gun is very helpful in preventing soldered wires from coming loose or being shorted out. You can get a light-duty one

and a bag of glue sticks from a craft store.

Wire strippers, knife, and needlenose pliers [G] These tools are necessary to prepare and shape the wires for soldering.

"Helping hands" (optional) [H] These are simply clips mounted on flexible arms that hold wires in the proper place while you solder. I made a pair using half of a RadioShack project box and some spare alligator clips.

Jumper wire kit [I] Sometimes it's difficult to solder the Cat 5 wires directly to the pins of the DB-15 connector or the TTL reader. For inexperienced solderers, I recommend soldering wires first to the connector and then to the reader before finally connecting them to the Cat 5. RadioShack part #276-173 is a good choice, and it'll cost you around $6. The kit is a necessity if you have to make a parallel port adapter.

Port adapter

Project box [J] RadioShack #270-283A is just what you want. It's a good size and comes with a small PC board and mounting screws. $4

Wire kit [I] If you didn't buy one for the first part of the project, you'll need one now. RadioShack #276-173.

9V Battery [K] $1

Octal buffer/line driver, 74541 [L] Since we are only protecting four inputs, a hex driver like a 74367 Hex Buffer would also work. Just make sure its non-inverting.

DB-15 Female connector [M] Available online.

DB-25 Male connector [N] Available online.

7805 Regulator [O] Converts our 12V into 5V needed by the buffer.

2 Capacitors [P] These should be rated for over 10V. The exact value of the capacitors doesn't matter. I used 10uF.

Red LED [Q]

Green LED [R]

1K ohm resistor [S]

Slide switch [T] Any kind of mini on-off switch will do.

9-Volt battery connector [U] "Snap-on" terminal type.

Dremel Tool [V] For cutting holes in the project box.

Needlenose pliers [W]

Hot glue gun [X]

Soldering iron and solder [Y]

Electrical tape [Z]

Not all items are shown in the image above.

MAKE IT.

BUILD YOUR MAGSTRIPE READER

START ⋰⋱   Time: **2 hrs.** Complexity: **Medium**

1. BUILDING THE BASIC MAGNETIC STRIPE READER

The central component of our project is a TTL magstripe reader. You don't want one that's advertised as being serial, parallel, keyboard, or USB based. Fortunately, TTL (also called "clock/data") readers are much cheaper than other readers because they don't contain circuitry for processing card data.

A TTL reader has three outputs: a card-present (CP) line, which lets you know when a card is being swiped; a clock (CLK) line, which goes high when the DATA line is valid; and a DATA line, which delivers a stream of ones and zeroes representing the data on the card. You will wire these signals to the pins of the game port. These pins are the same pins that joystick buttons use.

Basically, this reader "fools" your computer into thinking it is processing the activation of joystick buttons. First, the CP "button" is "pressed." Then the CLK button is pressed, which saves the state of the DATA button. This allows the Stripe Snoop software to capture the entire bitstream contained on the card and decode it.

1a. Prepare the connector. The first step is pretty easy. Take the DB-15 male connector and place it in your helping hands. Take a wire from your jumper wire kit and place it in the other helping hand. Maneuver the wire so that it sits in the hollow part of the pin, and solder the end to pin 2. Repeat for pins 4, 7, 14, and 15.

Next, cover the pins with hot glue to ensure the wires can't pull loose or touch each other.

Pins 4 and 15 correspond to ground (GND) and 5V, respectively, while pins 2, 7, and 14 are the buttons used by joysticks. It's easy to get turned around and forget which pin is which. Use a permanent marker to label the pins.

If you're new to soldering, be sure to check out our Primer article, *Soldering & Desoldering*, p. 162.

1b. Wire up the TTL reader. Use a knife to carefully remove the side panel that covers the Omron V3A-4's circuit board. Cut the farthest right tab off of the cover (the tab the knife is pointing to in this picture). This hole is where our wires will come out.

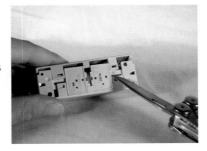

1c. At one end of the circuit board you should see a row of nine metal contacts. We will be soldering wires to pins 1, 2, 4, 5, and 6 (Contact 1 is at the bottom and 9 is at the top as seen here). These contacts are rather small, and it's easy to put down too much solder and short two of them together.

1d. Go slowly and make sure not to use too much solder. Check neighboring contacts as you go to make sure they don't touch. Also check to ensure that you can see the white line in between them. If not, use the soldering iron to heat both contacts, remove the excess solder with a solder sucker, and try again.

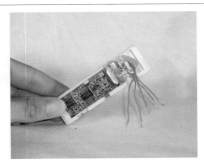

This is the hardest part of the project. If you keep shorting the contacts together, try using the soldering iron to melt a small amount of solder onto the contact. It should bead easily and not touch the neighboring contact. Now, holding the wire in one hand and the soldering iron in the other, heat the bead of solder and push the wire into the liquid metal.

1e. Once each wire is soldered, carefully bend it 90 degrees and position it so that it exits the back of the reader where we previously removed the tab from the side cover. Use the hot glue gun on the bent wires when you are done to make sure they don't pull loose. Be careful that you don't use so much glue that you can't see which wire is soldered to which pin. It is useful to fan out the wires (as shown) to keep the order correct.

Be careful bending the wires to ensure that you don't pull apart the soldered connections. Use a pair of needlenose pliers to hold the wires steady at the solder joint before bending them with your fingers.

1f. Connect the reader and connector.
The hard stuff is behind us. Now we simply join the DB-15 connector and the reader. Take your four-foot piece of Cat 5 cable and pick five wires you want to use. I recommend using all four of the solid color wires, and one of the striped wires. Strip off about 1.5 inches of insulation from each end. Cut off the three wires you are not using so that they don't get in the way, and strip a quarter-inch off each of the five wires you are using. Do this to both ends of the cable. We are going to connect the pins of the TTL reader to the pins of the DB-15 connector as indicated below.

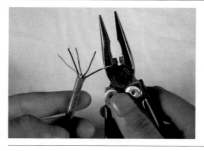

Pinout for Card Reader and DB-15 Connector

Omron V3A pin	DB-15 pin	Cat 5 cable color	Purpose
1	4	Brown	GND
2	15	Orange	5V
4	14	Green/white	CP
5	7	Blue	CLK
6	2	Green	DATA

1g. Use pliers to make small hooks at the end of each wire coming from the reader, connector, and cable.
Hook the correct wires together and use a little bit of solder to secure them.

While this step is not technically demanding, it is quite easy to make a mistake. It is very important that you solder the correct wires together. For each connection, I would solder one end of the jumper wire to the reader and the other to the DB-15 before moving on to the next wire. This helps prevent mistakes.

Use a small piece of electrical tape to protect each junction. Once complete, use more electrical tape to strengthen the transition at each end of the Cat 5.

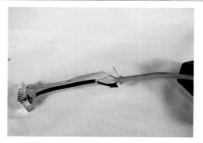

Zip ties and heat-shrink tubing can help clean this up and make it look more professional.

2. BUILDING A PARALLEL PORT ADAPTER

So what do you do if your computer doesn't have a game port? Well, as long as you have an available parallel port, you can build a simple adapter that allows you to use the reader we have constructed.

The adapter makes use of the five inputs used by printers to report errors to the PC. Instead of checking if the CLK joystick "button" is pressed and saving the status of the DATA button, we are checking to see if the printer is out of paper, and then saving the status of the acknowledge pin. We use a buffer/line driver chip between the game port and the parallel port to protect against future readers that might produce too much current and damage the parallel port. We also need a 5V power supply because the parallel port doesn't have one.

2a. Prepare the project box. Use a Dremel tool to cut the holes in the project box. I'll refer to the face where the metal plate goes as the top of the box. Place the box top down, so you are looking at the bottom face, with the short sides to the east and west. On the east side of the bottom face, drill a ⅛" hole. This is for our battery leads.

Now, on the west face of the box, near its edge with the bottom face, cut a hole for the DB-15 connector. It should just fit between the two screw posts. Remember: don't glue any of these components in yet!

On the south face (a long side), near the edge it forms with the bottom face, cut a hole for our DB-25 connector. We want this hole to be close to the west side of the face, about ½" from the edge the south and west faces make. Again, use the Dremel to cut a hole and then shape it until the DB-25 connection fits.

Finally, we need to cut holes for our power switch and power LED. These go on the east face, near the edge the east and bottom faces make. Drill a ⅛" hole for the LED's wires, and use the Dremel to make a small hole for the power switch.

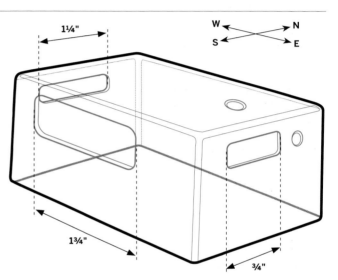

This is going to be messy! Do this in a place that is easy to vacuum. Wear eye protection against the flying plastic pieces.

2b. Prepare the connectors. Next we need to prepare our DB-15, DB-25, power switch, and LED. Since these components will be mounted to the project box, it's important the wires we solder to them are long enough for us to comfortably solder them to the circuit board. You should use the longer wires in the wire kit. We are going to solder long wires (the red wires are a good length) to pins 2, 4, 7, 10, 14, and 15 on the DB-15 connector. After you're done, use the hot glue gun and cover all the pins and wires.

Solder wires to the DB-25 pins 10, 11, 12, 13, 15, and 25. Again, use the longer wires to give yourself enough slack. Use the hot glue gun to cover all exposed metal on the back of the connector.

For the power switch and LED, solder wires to the leads on both. Make sure you remember which wire is attached to the shorter lead on the LED. This wire will later be connected to GND.

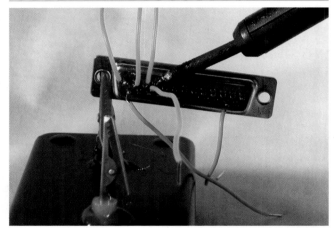

The pin numbers on the DB-15 female connector are the reverse of the male connector. Use a permanent marker and note which pins are which! Do the same for the DB-25.

2c: Make the power supply. The power supply should be located on the left side of the circuit board. Don't worry about soldering on the battery leads yet, so be sure to leave some space to the left of the power supply. Use the shortest wires from the wire kit: red, orange, yellow, and green. When connecting components, twist the leads together using a pair of needlenose pliers. The circuit is rather straightforward, as shown in the diagram. There are a lot of connections to the power supply's outputs (especially GND) so leave room around them. Try not to have more than four wires at each junction. As you need to, use short red wires to extend a junction for additional wires. Note that the lead on the capacitor closest to the off-color stripe, or the lead that is the shortest, should be connected to GND.

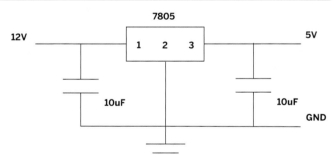

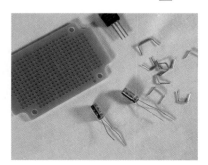

Hint: If it makes you more comfortable, build this circuit on a breadboard first. Then implement it in stages.

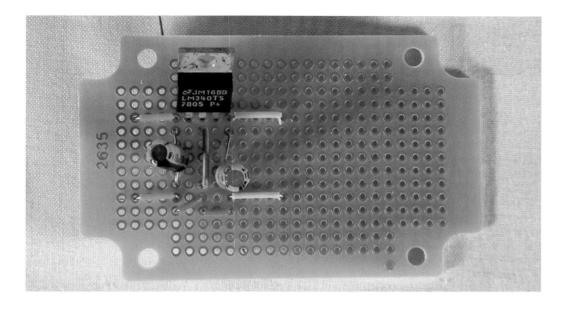

2d. Attach the octal buffer, final preparations. With the power supply on the left of the circuit board, place the 74541 chip on the right side of the board, with about five holes open to its right. You should also place the chip upside down (pin 1 at the bottom). This places our input pins (pins 2-5) on the right, where the DB-15 connector will be. Solder the 5V and GND wires to the pins as shown. Attach the resistor to a 5V line and leave the end open. We will connect this to our power LED.

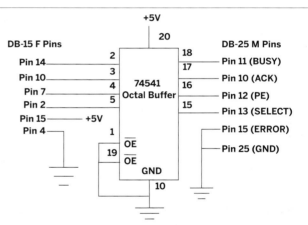

Bend the unused pins on the 74541 to help hold the chip to the board while soldering. Just make sure you don't let any of them touch.

2e. Final construction. Now we attach the wired connectors to the circuit board. Push the power switch into its hole, with the wires going into the box. Use hot glue to secure it in place. Do the same with the LED. Slide both leads from the battery-clip thru hole in the bottom face and solder the black wire of the battery clip to the GND input of the power supply. Solder one end of the power switch to the 9V input of the power supply and the other to the red wire of the battery clip. Solder the wire on the short side of the LED to the GND and the other to the resistor.

Don't use too much glue with the power switch, or you could glue the switch into one position. Things will get difficult as you attach the wires from both DB connectors. Make sure in all the mess you don't short anything out.

Next, glue the DB-25 connector into place. Solder the pins to the correct pins of the octal buffer using the circuit diagram. Remember, the octal buffer is upside down; all the DB-25 wires should connect to the side of the chip facing the power supply. Solder them according to the diagram.

Finally, slide and glue the DB-15 connector into place. Things are probably getting crowded, so use needle-nose pliers to help move the wires into position. Solder them according to the diagram.

Usage and notes. Sometimes, if the adapter is connected to the parallel port and the battery is not connected, the power light will still be on. I'm still not entirely sure why this happens. Depending on the amps needed to run your reader, it may even function. However, to guarantee the results, use a battery. The circuit will also operate without a buffer chip. However, it's better to fry a 50-cent part than your parallel port. Use the chip.

Please note: A black box with wires coming out of it, a switch, and a red light tends to worry airport security. You have been warned!

FINISH X

NOW GO USE IT »

USING THE STRIPE SNOOP SOFTWARE

```
Opening "/dev/ttyS0"
Reading from /dev/ttyS0
Decoding...

Track 1: %B4313^05041000000?
Track 2: ;4313=050410100000?

Found a Visa Credit Card

Issued To: Harold Diddlebock
Account Number: 43 130 50155
Expires: April 2008
Encrypted PIN: 5673
Issuing Bank: Maryland Bank (MBNA)
```

STRIPE SNOOP (*stripesnoop.sf.net*), released under the GPL, is a program for both Linux and Windows. While it is command-line based, GUI front ends are in a preliminary development stage. Installation is very straightforward and the program comes equipped with a lot of documentation that is also available on the website.

A few notes and limitations: due to the way Stripe Snoop accesses hardware, you will need to run it as root if you are running Linux. Due to the polling nature of the game port, please run Stripe Snoop on a machine faster than a Pentium 200 that isn't heavily loaded with other programs. Currently, Stripe Snoop is only functional on x86 architecture although a USB-based reader is in the development stage.

There is a simple program, rdetect, which will help configure Stripe Snoop for your reader. Once setup, run Stripe Snoop using the command ss. When prompted, swipe your card. Using different ISO standards, Stripe Snoop will try to decode the bitstream it captures from your newly built hardware interface and display the data to the screen. If the card is in its built-in database, it will supply more meaningful information to the screen than just the raw data stream.

For instance, the stream "4313012345678901= 05061010000565" would be decoded by Stripe Snoop as a Visa Credit Card issued by MBNA with such-and-such credit number and expiration date. Stripe Snoop has several features including a raw mode, which allows you to see the card's bitstream, and a force mode, which will (try to) parse damaged magstripes. There are several other options available, and I encourage you to read the documentation.

You can read all three tracks on your cards by making simple shims to insert into the card stripe reader. Find out how to do this on my website: *stripesnoop.sourceforge.net/mod.html*.

FUTURE PROJECT IDEAS

Cola machine: Now that you have a system to read an account number from a card, causing an action based on the account number is the next logical step. I built a cola machine that releases soda using motors and relays when its reads my student ID. This is certainly a fun project, and shows how magstripes can function in a larger project. Visit Most Significant Bit Labs (*www.msblabs.org*) for more information.

Power LED: Is this thing on? A power LED built into the reader is fairly easy to do and very helpful. Perhaps you hook it up to the parallel port and use it to provide feedback about a swipe (blink if it didn't parse, green if good, etc.).

Toss the PC: There's no reason you have to use a PC and Stripe Snoop to decode the magstripe. PIC, BasicStamp, and other microcontrollers are perfectly capable of doing it, too. This will help keep your project small. If you do need to use a computer, there is an older DOS version of Stripe Snoop that can run on a 386, and I've gotten the Linux version to work on a 486 running Slackware. Visit Stripe Snoop's homepage for information on the magstripe standards and source code.

USB Reader: What about a USB-based interface? A simple microcontroller to collect all the information and a cheap USB chipset could be the basis of the next generation of readers.

Bruce Sterling

MAKE THE TOOLS THAT MADE YOU

Flintknappers reveal our technological origins, one chip at a time.

HANDMADE TOOLS ARE TWO MILLION YEARS old. Modern humans are just 200,000 years old. Before we humans came along, our Stone Age ancestors spent 1,800,000 years making tools out of rocks.

It follows that you, a modern human, have evolved superb eyes and hands for that job. If you invest some thought and effort, you'll find that you can make much better Stone Age tools than a Stone Age guy.

Genuine Stone Agers often had to trudge dozens of miles to dig up flint with prehistoric shovels of antler and bone. Today's sophisticated stone maker can order rock supplies shipped by FedEx. You can even have stone neatly prepared for you into arrowhead-sized blanks, so you can concentrate on the fun part of stonework, which is "knapping."

Top-class stone hackers give public classes and shoot how-to videos. They call themselves "master knappers" and hang out with museum curators and archaeologists.

The Purist Approach

There are basically three schools of knapping. The first, and most honored, is "abo knapping" — the purist approach that uses only natural, prehistoric tools and techniques. The high concept is to re-create the Stone Age lifestyle with a scholarly understanding of prehistoric skills.

An ideal abo knapper would thrive if dropped naked in a wilderness. He would find a suitably brittle rock and crack it open with a cobble — this cracking process is referred to as "spalling."

Then he would knock long shards from the freshly cracked edge (known as "percussion flaking") and sharpen and refine the edges by peeling and prying off bits with a pointy piece of bone — called "pressure flaking." He would then smooth out a wooden stick, carefully notch the stone blade, and haft that into the tip.

At this point, the abo knapper has created a Stone Age throwing spear. After his first kill, he's got sinew, blood glue, a loincloth, bone tools, a canteen, some rawhide sandals, and basically everything he needs besides a cave-art gallery.

Entrepreneurial Market Knappers

The second school is referred to as "market knapping." Here you find the guys who make modern arrowheads, stone knives, and custom spearheads for the joy of it and for the tourist trade. These guys tend to be congenial folklorists, hobby hunters, and local craftsmen.

The Flintknapping Avant-Garde

The members of the last and rarest school of knappers have a different perspective: they use engineering terms like "conchoidal fracture" and are into high-performance stonework. They will knap most anything, including semiprecious stones, broken pop bottles, busted toilet bowls, telephone insulators, and the billets of purified silica used to make fiber-optic cables. These avant-gardists tend to be jewelers and rock hounds.

Not for the Weak

Knapping is serious, hands-on work. It takes patience and some muscle in the shoulders and forearms, and it requires vigorous pounding, prying, and chipping on brittle, glassy materials that can pop off and fly at high velocities. Assuming that you preserve your eyesight (always a great idea), you'll still have to manage the safety of your fingers and your feet. If you wonder whether stone weapons hurt, just ask a mammoth.

Bruce Sterling (bruce@well.com) is a science fiction writer and part-time design professor.

Photograph courtesy of Piltdown Productions, Lynchburg, VA

CRACK OPEN AN iPAQ

Replacing your PDA's battery requires the proper knowledge, adequate courage, and a set of Torx screwdrivers. By Dale Dougherty

While I was getting a new home theater installed, the installer asked if I used a Pocket PC. He said I could make it function as an additional remote control. I had an early model iPAQ, but stopped using it for a number of reasons and it was confined to a closet. The iPAQ is a slim, beautiful device and one of the first color PDAs. I used it as an MP3 player for music and audio books. I also bought TravRoute CoPilot, a GPS navigation system for the Pocket PC that never quite worked for me.

I recalled that my iPAQ's battery no longer held a charge. Batteries are a headache. My Sony digital camera, which is less than a year old, has a rechargeable battery that has started to fail; the time remaining on the battery went from 30 minutes to zero in practically no time! At least I can buy a new battery and easily swap out the old one. No tools required.

Not so with an iPAQ (or an iPod, for that matter.) The design pre-supposes you will eventually replace the entire device, not just its battery. In other words, you'll upgrade for new features before you

> You have to crack open the iPAQ to remove the battery, which is glued to the cover.

Torque on the Cheap: Eklind 7-Piece Torx Fold-Up Key Set from J&L Industrial Supply, about $10.

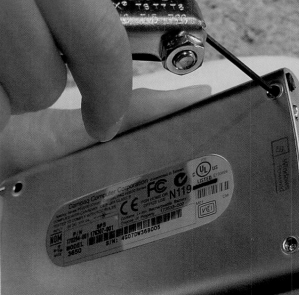

A lot of consumer electronics devices use Torx screws, so it's smart to have a set of Torx drivers in your toolbox.

The first step, removing the screws from the iPAQ, is also the easiest. The next steps require a degree of delicacy to complete.

wear it out. But my iPAQ was sitting in a closet in hopes that some day I would find a specialized use for it that would make me retrieve it from the discard pile.

I used Google to see if I could learn how to replace the battery myself. Now, I must confess that I'm not particularly handy nor do I have an innate curiosity about the internals of a device. In fact, as I looked into the problem, I discovered I was missing a basic tool that would allow me to open an iPAQ: a Torx screwdriver.

Finding the Battery and a Torx Screwdriver

Torx screws are star-shaped and come in numerous sizes. I needed a set of Torx screwdrivers rather than a single one because I had to match the specific size, much as you would with an Allen wrench. The iPAQ uses T6 screws. I noticed a few weeks earlier that my Titanium PowerBook was put together with Torx screws (they were slightly larger T8s). A newer aluminum PowerBook uses T6 screws. Also, if you plan to hack into a TiVo box, you'll encounter T10 and T15 screws.

I found a fold-up Torx key set on Amazon for about $10. It had seven different sizes (T6, T7, T8, T10, T11, T12, T14). I could have bought individual screwdrivers and paid a little more or a little less. I chose the key set, which folds up like a Swiss Army knife, because I thought it might be easier to locate in a drawer instead of several really small Torx screwdrivers.

Using Google, I found instructions for replacing the battery at *PDAparts.com*, which also sold the battery. The replacement battery cost $65 and it arrived in the mail within several days. I then set out to remove the back cover from the iPAQ.

Opening the iPAQ

Once I removed the four T6 screws, the back cover remained tightly in place. Removing it felt a bit like I was cracking open a crab shell. I poked at a seam with a knife and got it open just slightly. Cracking it all the way open required more effort and I wasn't sure if I was damaging the insides, especially since there was a cracking sound. Soon, though, I had two halves of an iPAQ. The battery is actually glued to the back inside cover of the case.

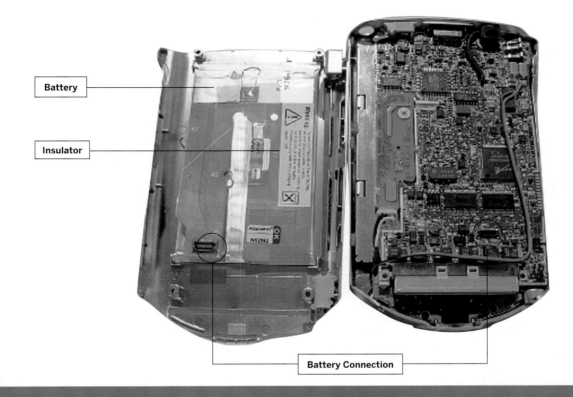

Battery

Insulator

Battery Connection

Now the instructions said to open the case slowly because — as I found out later when I went back and reread the procedure — the battery is attached to the motherboard, and once you get it open, you are supposed to detach the small battery connector. When I forced open the case, the connector came off immediately.

Replacing the Battery and Closing the iPAQ

I removed the old battery easily from its glue mounts, and those mounts remained sufficiently sticky to secure the new battery in place. The hardest part for me was actually connecting the battery back to the motherboard. The connector is very small and it's awkward to place the attachment on the connector itself. I put the back on but did not replace the screws until I had tested the battery.

On my first attempt I did not have the battery attached properly. When I put the iPAQ in its holder to charge and then removed it, the battery didn't work. I thought perhaps I had broken something while taking apart the iPAQ. I took apart the iPAQ again and tried to fit the attachment

into the tiny connector, taking more care than I had previously. This time, as soon as I made the proper connection, the iPAQ turned on and lit up. So I knew it worked. I recharged it overnight and then replaced the screws.

The next day I called my AV installer to tell him I had a Pocket PC ready to go.

Dale Dougherty is editor and publisher of MAKE.

iPaqs On Ebay

I found my exact model on eBay selling for about $150. There was a non-working model with a cracked screen (parts-only) selling for $5.99. Newer models were $200 and up.

The iPAQ was developed by Compaq, which has since been acquired by Hewlett-Packard. I visited the HP support website and found information about the model iPAQ I owned, but I could not easily find information about replacing the battery nor about parts. The entry-level model iPAQ on the HP site costs $279 and there are models in the $400 and $600 range.

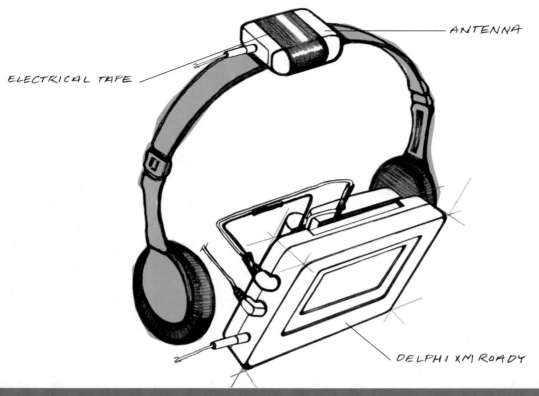

ANTENNA

ELECTRICAL TAPE

DELPHI XM ROADY

PORTABLE SATELLITE RADIO

Portable satellite radio makes the Delphi XM Roady ready to wear. By Dave Mathews

As much as I am a fan of the iTunes music store, I prefer satellite radio for its brainless ease of use. You might consider them two different forms of media distribution: satellite music is push to the Apple Music Store's pull. With push, your $10 monthly satellite fee gets you thousands of songs automatically. With pull, the same amount gets you only ten 99-cent songs from iTunes that you must click to find, download, store and sync. And you need to know the name of the song or artist, too. Unless you have extremely eclectic music taste, iTunes can rarely beat the kind of professional programming found on an XM station. Finally, you could never get live CNN or weather on your iPod.

I've been using a Delphi XM Roady to listen to satellite music in my car. But it's not as portable as my iPod. I wanted my XM Roady to be wearable

and have it go where I go. So I set out to modify the antenna and devise a lightweight power supply using AA batteries. A quick trip to RadioShack provided nearly all of the necessary gear to solve my problem.

Adapt the Antenna

The Delphi Roady comes with its own antenna, but a better choice is the new XMicro aerial from Terk. This $29 antenna is nearly half the size of the original, making it much easier to wear.

I attached the antenna to the headphones with electrical tape. Satellite signals have no problem passing through non-metallic tape and the antenna

It's not hard to convert an XM Roady satellite radio receiver into a handheld portable unit.

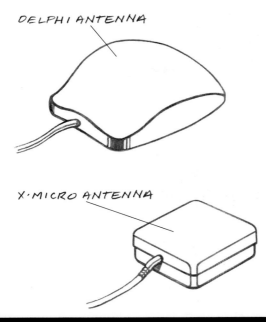

DELPHI ANTENNA

X·MICRO ANTENNA

BATTERY PACK

The XMicro aerial from Terk (bottom) is about half the size of the antenna that comes with the XM Roady, making it a better choice for personal use.

Connect a quad AA battery holder to a single AA holder and wire them in series terminating at a "Type B" Adaptaplug.

wire can be routed alongside the headphone audio cable.

Because the XMicro antenna is designed to plug into a trunk-mounted XM tuner, I had to modify its connector by removing the pink plastic connector shroud. I used a small screwdriver to get between the white and pink plastic and gently extract the white plastic locking piece. Then I heat-shrank a "strain relief" over the top of the connector and the exposed wire to keep things neat and prevent the wire from breaking. This rubber "shrinky dink" tubing will contract tightly over the wires once you apply heat from a hair dryer to it. Unless you are an RF engineer, the antenna coax cable should not be cut or spliced, as it is tuned specifically to receive combined satellite and terrestrial broadcasts.

Create a Power Supply

Next, I had to create a 6-volt power supply. Whether you plan on using alkaline batteries which output 1.5 Volts or rechargeable batteries with 1.2 Volt capacity, it is best to use 5 AA cells to make sure you have sufficient current to run the audio amplifier. I connected a four AA battery holder in series with a single AA holder to garner 6 to 9 volts, which is well within tolerances for the receiver. By comparison, the iPod Lithium Ion battery is just 3.7 volts; but its chassis, including battery, is nearly the same dimension as the XM Roady tuner without the battery bundle.

To wire the battery packs, I took the red wire from the single AA battery holder and connected it to the black wire from the quad AA holder. I soldered these wires together and heat-shrank the splice to prevent any short circuits. Next, I had to attach the remaining wires to a plug that matched the power port of the Roady. I used a RadioShack Adaptaplug "Type B" tip and connected the red wire from the quad AA holder to the left post of the tip as it sits on its back with the "+" facing me. The black wire from the single AA battery holder went to the right tip connector. You can tape or shrink wrap the solder points and insert batteries into the holders. I used a volt meter to check that there was no more than 9 volts with positive voltage at the tip – inside the hole. Then I plugged in the antenna connector to the Roady. You can use a fanny pack or rubber band to bind the battery holders and Roady together.

D.I.Y. HOME ENTERTAINMENT

Ready to Wear

At this point the unit was ready to be turned on, but I didn't want to use the power button. Using the power button to turn the unit off and on will turn on the display's LEDs, eating up battery power. Instead, input the sequence "232" into the keypad and then push in the scroll wheel on the side. This undocumented "Easter egg" will power up the Roady without lighting any LEDs and will save battery life. Unfortunately, you must power up with this method every time in order to eliminate the backlight — this is not a "sticky" or non-volatile setting.

Since the Roady has only a line-level output, I chose headphones that have an in-line volume switch. To get the most volume output from the Roady, I pressed the Menu button and scrolled down to Audio Level and pressed the wheel in. At the level screen, I rolled the wheel all the way to the right, then pressed the wheel in to set the level to 9. With the Roady now outputting full volume, I could then use the headphone in-line control to tame the music coming out of the beast.

The Roady Meets the Sidewalk

I plugged in the headphones and headed outside. Depending on where I roamed, I could sometimes get away with placing the antenna inside a fanny pack out of sky view. Your mileage will definitely vary. I live just outside of the repeater network and find that placing the antenna on my head helps improve reception around trees and other complex terrain.

By the time you read this, a new second generation Roady2 should be available which uses new low power chips for an even longer portable playback time! Take a look at the Easter eggs (sidebar) for even more tweaking and signal strength monitoring. Enjoy your virtually unlimited portable music library!

Dave Mathews (www.davemathews.com) lives in Dallas where he broadcasts as the "Gadget Guy" on TV and radio.

PARTS LIST:
Terk XMicro Antenna $29
RadioShack Adaptaplug "B" power tip 273-1705 $4.99
RadioShack 4XAA Battery Holder 270-391 $1.69
RadioShack 1XAA Battery Holder 270-401 $0.99
RadioShack Over-the-head Headphones with Volume Control 33-1116 $9.99
RadioShack Heat-Shrink Tubing 278-1627 $2.39
Rubber Bands

EQUIPMENT NEEDED:
Small Flathead Screwdriver
Electrical Tape
Wire Ties
Volt Meter

XM Easter Eggs:

You can access some undocumented features of the XM Roady by entering the codes and clicking the scroll wheel:

123 Demo Mode
211 Reset Presets
226 Diagnostics
232 Turn on without LEDS

SDARS Reception

SDARS (Satellite Digital Audio Radio Services) satellites are in a 22,300-mile geostationary orbit in space and are augmented with some 1,500 terrestrial repeaters in the 2.33 GHz airspace. This repeater network helps to eliminate "building fade" that may block the satellite signals coming from 85 and 115 West degree slots from reaching tuners on Earth. Depending upon how close you are to the repeaters, you may not even need a "sky view" to get good reception. And if you are lucky, you can receive a signal indoors.

Related Sites:

ID XM Repeaters
http://www.telebeans.org/telco/towers/notes/xm_radio.html

XM Tutorial
http://www.wave-report.com/Tutorials/XM.htm

XM Technical Specs
http://www.tvtower.com/xm-radio.html

XM Easter Eggs
http://www.xm411.com/phpbb/viewtopic.php?t=2073

Lost photo rescued by CameraSalvage.

UNZAP FLASH MEMORY

How to salvage deleted pictures from camera memory. By Mark Frauenfelder

When I was in Japan for a few days last year, I took a lot of pictures of people wearing uniforms. It seemed like everyone in Tokyo, from leaf raker to hair stylist to vending machine mechanic, was wearing a slick-looking uniform.

When I got back to my hotel room after a day of shooting, I was eager to upload the photos to my iBook so I could post them to my blog. I plugged my digital camera into my computer, started uploading photos, and when the process was complete, no photos were there! Worse, the photos on my memory card were gone.

I wrote it off as bad luck and went out to take more pictures. When I got back, I emailed a friend and told him what had happened. He said, "Don't take any more pictures!" He told me to try CameraSalvage, an application specifically designed to recover photographs that were deleted from flash memory cards by mistake.

It turns out that flash memory stores data much like a hard drive. When a file is erased, it's really the directory, not the file, that's deleted.

Since I had already taken several pictures after the disaster, I didn't have much hope of recovering the uniform shots, but I gave it a try.

Fingers crossed, I fired up the application. CameraSalvage filled a folder with most of the photos I'd lost. I haven't had an occasion to use the application again, and I hope I never will, but it's nice knowing I have it in case things go wrong.

CameraSalvage: $40, *www.SubRosaSoft.com*

Mark Frauenfelder is editor-in-chief of MAKE.

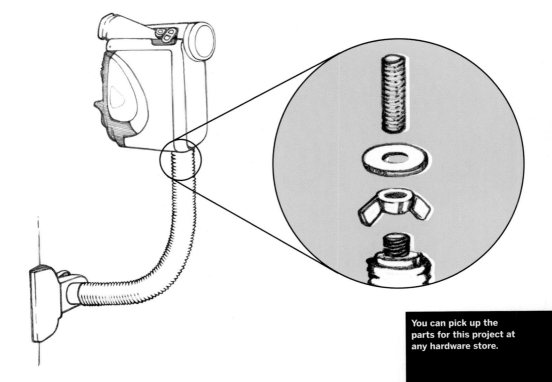

You can pick up the parts for this project at any hardware store.

FLEXIBLE GOOSENECK CAMERA MOUNT

Put a camera or camcorder pretty much anywhere with this flexible camera mount built from a cheap desk lamp. By Marc H. Nathan

This little item should be a welcome addition to your camera gear. It will clip to the back of the seat in front of you so you can tape your kid's school play, or on a rolled-down car window to take the hard work out of your obligatory summer-trip family photo.

All it takes is a gooseneck lamp that can be bought new for less than $10 (but it's much more satisfying to salvage one), and a bare minimum of hardware.

This can be done in a number of ways, including the use of epoxy and solder, but the easiest method is to screw the bolt into the threads of the lamp neck. Cut off the bolt head, add the wing nut and washer, and attach the camera equipment.

MATERIALS:	OPTIONAL:
1 Gooseneck lamp with clamp	Dremel tool – To cut off bolt head
1" Bolt	Epoxy or solder kit – To attach bolt to lamp neck
1" Wing nut	
1" Washer	

Directions:

Remove all lamp hardware and the power cable from the lamp. Attach the bolt to the lamp neck.

Marc Nathan is an angel investor and technology enthusiast who lives with his wife and two bulldogs in Houston, Texas.

USING A HIGH-SPEED WIRELESS CARD

Would you sacrifice a few meals each month for wireless networking away from home?

By Brian Jepson

Back when I was still tethering my computers to a router, I pulled out a really long 10BaseT cable whenever I wanted to use my laptop in the living room. Around the same time that I started sniffing around catalogs for Wi-Fi equipment, I discovered that Verizon Wireless was offering CDPD (Cellular Digital Packet Data). It was cheap — $40 a month for unlimited data; but it was slow — 19.2Kbps (kilobits per second).

It wasn't long before I gave in and spent the money on a home Wi-Fi network. But I kept the CDPD because it offered internet access any-

where I could get a cellular signal. It's been years since Verizon Wireless offered CDPD, and I've graduated to faster experiences: first GPRS, then EDGE, and now something called 1xRTT/1xEV-DO (all described below).

Cellular Data Services

Here's a rundown of all the data services I've tested and who offers them. I've used

For EV-DO, I use Verizon Wireless Broadband with the Audiovox PC5220 PC Card.

(at various times) Sprint (*www.pcsvision.com*), Verizon Wireless (*www.verizonwireless.com*), AT&T Wireless (*www.attwireless.com*), and T-Mobile (*www.t-mobile.com*).

GPRS

General Packet Radio Services (AT&T Wireless, T-Mobile, Cingular). This protocol hitches a ride on GSM (Global System for Mobile communications), a voice technology that can fit as much as 13.2Kbps into a timeslot.

EDGE

Enhanced Data rates for GSM Evolution (AT&T Wireless, Cingular). This technology lets GSM network operators cram more data into timeslots.

1xRTT

Single Carrier (1x) Radio Transmission Technology (Sprint, Verizon Wireless). This is part of the CDMA (Code Division Multiple Access) family of cellular communications. CDMA makes a provision for up to 144Kbps per user.

1xEV-DO

Single Carrier Evolution Data Only (Verizon Wireless). This is also part of the CDMA family, but kicks the data rate up quite a bit.

Getting Started

Verizon Wireless is the only major carrier in the United States to offer 1xEV-DO. If you check out the Verizon Wireless site, you'll find a bewildering array of data plans. Some of these plans (per minute and per megabyte plans) apply to the NationalAccess service, which only gets you 1xRTT. If you want to be able to use both 1xRTT and 1xEV-DO, you'll need the Unlimited NationalAccess and BroadbandAccess plan, which is $79.99 a month and does not include any voice time.

You can sign up for the service online or in a Verizon Wireless or authorized dealer's store. Go to the store first: you might get a better deal than the ones offered on the Verizon Wireless website. Whether you go to a store or buy it online, there will almost always be a discount and rebate, and it will be bigger if you sign up for a two-year plan. Do the math, and assume you're going to cancel after a year. This gives you a worst-case scenario

you can use to decide whether to sign up for a two-year or a one-year contract.

Contract Length	1 year	2 years
Price of the Card	$299.99	$249.99
Activation Fee	$35.00	$15.00
Rebate	$150.00	$150.00
Early Termination Fee	$0.00	$175.00

So, if you terminate your service after one year, the one-time costs are $184.99 with a one-year contract. But, if you terminate after one year on a two-year contract, the one-time costs are $289.99. If you stick it out with the two-year contract, it's only $114.99.

Use an Antenna

I don't get a signal at home. I don't get a signal on the train between Providence and South Station. In fact, the PC5220 PC card adapter that I use in my laptop to get EV-DO service has a very bad reputation for signal strength in 1xRTT mode. And I spend most of my time in 1xRTT territory. So I went in search of an external antenna, and found I needed two things: the antenna itself, and an adapter to connect the antenna to my PC5220.

The antenna I chose is a Patch Glass Mount Antenna with Suction Cups (part CA09-1G, $25) from *www.cellantenna.com*. I found the adapter I needed, an Antenna Adapter Cable, PC3200/PC3220/PC5220, FME (SKU 421575, $22), from *www.yourwirelesssource.com*. After plugging the antenna into my EV-DO card, I was able to receive a signal at home and on the train.

Of all the data plans I've tried, Verizon Wireless' 1xRTT/1xEV-DO combo is my favorite. In most circumstances, it operates at 1xRTT speeds. But I've got the billing statements to show how useful this has been: whether I was trapped in a hotel with no internet access or stuck at a conference with sluggish Wi-Fi, 1xRTT has had my back.

Note: The PC5220 comes with drivers for Windows. Mac OS X 10.3.5 and later includes drivers for this card, and an installer is available at *www.apple.com/support/downloads/verizonbroadbandaccess-support.html*. Linux users can find configuration information at *www.ka9q.net/5220.html*.

Brian Jepson is an O'Reilly editor, programmer, and co-author of three O'Reilly Media books.

PERFORMANCE OF SELECT DATA CARDS

Maximum and average data rates obtained
through field tests (Kbps).

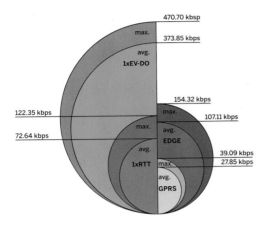

- 470.70 kbsp — max.
- 373.85 kbps — avg. 1xEV-DO
- 154.32 kbps — max.
- 122.35 kbps — max.
- 107.11 kbps — avg. EDGE
- 72.64 kbps — avg.
- 39.09 kbps — max.
- 27.85 kbps — avg. GPRS
- 1xRTT

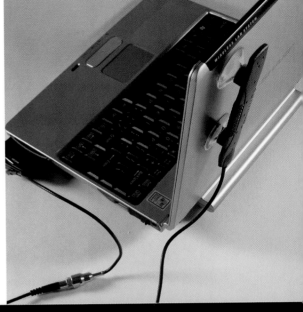

With the antenna and adapter
connected to my PC5220 card, I
can get a signal where there was
none before.

Debunking the WiMAX Hype
It's not long-range Wi-Fi (at least, not yet).

1xEV-DO is but one of many wireless technologies
that can spray packets far and wide. For example,
people have done line-of-sight Wi-Fi over distances
of 20 miles and more. One emerging technology
that's gotten a lot of press is WiMAX (*www.wimax-
forum.org/home*), but there's as much confusion
about WiMAX as there is buzz. WiMAX is based
on IEEE 802.16 (*www.ieee802.org/16/*), a wireless
standard for creating Metropolitan Area Networks
(MANs). Don't think of WiMAX or 802.16 as a base
station-to-laptop solution, or even a tower-to-lap-
top solution; its proponents, particularly Intel, are
pushing it as more of a tower-to-rooftop solution.
A single WiMAX tower can serve dozens of customers at speeds rivaling a T1. Once the service reaches
the customer, the customer uses a wired and/or
wireless LAN to distribute the bandwidth to users.
WiMAX is a last-mile solution — it addresses the
question of how to distribute bandwidth to users
once you've hauled a fat pipe out to a central location. This is not to say you couldn't outfit a laptop
with a WiMAX-capable wireless card; it's theoreti-
cally possible, and it's on the WiMAX roadmap. But
that's certainly not where the companies dabbling
in WiMAX are currently focused.

Where It Works: Cities

You won't get the screaming 1xEV-DO speeds
everywhere in the United States right now; most
of the country is still on 1xRTT. As of this writing,
Verizon Wireless has support for 1xEV-DO in the
following cities:

Atlanta, GA	Milwaukee, WI
Austin, TX	New Orleans, LA
Baltimore, MD	New York, NY
Dallas, TX	Philadelphia, PA
Fort Lauderdale, FL	San Diego, CA
Kansas City, MO	Tampa, FL
Las Vegas, NV	Washington, DC
Los Angeles, CA	West Palm Beach, FL
Miami, FL	

Where It Works: Airports

Dallas/Ft. Worth, TX (DFW)
Dallas/Love Field, TX (DAL)
Intercontinental Airport Houston, TX (IAH)
Houston/Hobby, TX (HOU)
Jacksonville International, FL (JAX)
Louis Armstrong New Orleans Intl., LA (MSY)
Orlando International, FL (MCO)
Phoenix Sky Harbor International, AZ (PHX)

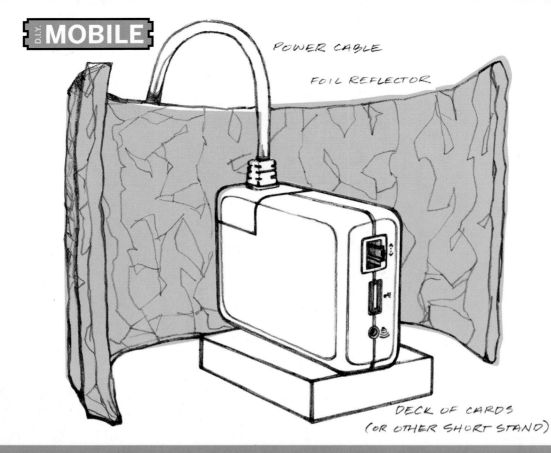

POWER CABLE

FOIL REFLECTOR

DECK OF CARDS
(OR OTHER SHORT STAND)

EXTENDING THE RANGE OF THE AIRPORT EXPRESS

Tips for getting the most out of a weak Wi-Fi signal. By Rob Flickenger

The first great curse of wireless networks is that they are not yet available on every square inch of the planet. The second great curse is that they are not always free to use. When traveling, it can be more than a little disappointing to use free wireless access in the city all day, only to return to your hotel room and be expected to pay $10 for in-room internet access.

There could be dozens of free networks lurking just outside your hotel room, barely out of range of your wireless laptop. If you only had a repeater and a good antenna, you could greatly extend your range and easily connect to a free network, instead of paying the captive audience fee

charged by some hotels. But who wants to pack all of that extra gear on a business trip?

Apple makes a wonderful little gadget called the AirPort Express. This box is just a little larger than a laptop power adapter and can act as a wireless client or repeater. With these simple tips, you can get much better range from the AirPort Express than you might expect.

1. Book a hotel room on a high floor facing the city. Your chances of finding an open network are much better

> You can boost your AirPort Express signal significantly with an aluminum foil reflector.

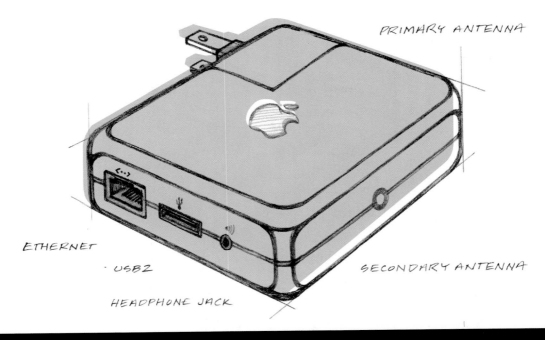

PRIMARY ANTENNA

ETHERNET

USB2

HEADPHONE JACK

SECONDARY ANTENNA

The AirPort Express has connector jacks for Ethernet, USB, and digital/ analog audio.

the higher you go, and having a window facing a large number of buildings is a must.

2. Swap the stubby power connector on the Express for the long cable on your laptop's power adapter. By using the long cord, you can more easily reposition the Express closer to the window, or wherever you can find the best possible signal.

3. If you can't find a network by moving the Air-Port Express, you can add an antenna. While adding a physically connected antenna is possible, it is very difficult without mangling the case of the AirPort Express. But you can easily take advantage of the gain provided by a passive reflector.

There are two antennas inside the AirPort Express. The primary antenna runs across the edge opposite the cable connectors. The secondary antenna lies along the same edge as the LED. If you place the primary antenna at the focal point of a metal reflector, you will get a better signal in the direction that the reflector points.

To make a reflector, you will need a piece of

flexible metal. If you're traveling, I highly recommend getting Indian take-out and saving the heavy aluminum foil the naan is wrapped in. Fold the foil into a roughly 6" x 8" rectangle. You should have enough foil to make it two or three layers thick. Smooth out the rectangle with a flat object (such as a book), then bend it into a gentle "C" shape. Place the AirPort Express on a short stand (such as a deck of cards) with the power cable sticking up. Now set the reflector about 2" behind the Express. Presto, you have gain in the direction that the reflector is pointing.

Now configure the Express for Wireless Distribution System (WDS), and select an available network from the list. If you still don't see a useable network, try moving the Express around and repositioning the reflector. If you can't find a good network for WDS, try configuring it to join a wireless network and connect the CAT5 port to your laptop. If all else fails, you can still use the Express as an access point on the in-hotel wired network and create a free network on your floor.

Rob Flickenger is the author of three O'Reilly Media books, including *Building Wireless Community Networks*.

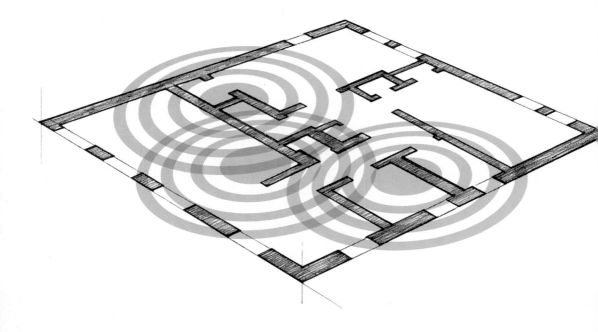

MESH NETWORKS WITH AIRPORT EXPRESS

How to break through concrete walls using Wireless Distribution mode. By Tom Bridge

When I moved into my condo a year ago, I was presented with a bit of a challenge: several of the interior walls were made of fairly thick concrete, and did a very good job of blocking out the Wi-Fi signal from the AirPort access point in the front of the house to the back. Consequently, for some time I dealt with cumbersome wires and a router sitting on my kitchen floor. It was not an ideal solution. Enter the AirPort Express — Apple's little 802.11g router, jukebox, and print server all rolled into one — and some serious tinkering.

AirPort Express in a Nutshell
At first glance, the AirPort Express appears much like the power adapter that ships with Apple lap-

tops: small and white, with a foldout, two-pronged plug. The bottom of the adapter contains three jacks: 10/100BASE-T Ethernet (for networking via DSL or cable modems or a local area network), USB (for wirelessly sharing a USB printer), and a ⅛"-inch audio-in (for home stereo). The AirPort Express ships with software, called the AirPort Express Assistant, to configure the device as an iTunes host, a print server, and a network device.

Overall the softare isn't much to work with; however, it will handle the basics to get you going. The new AirPort Admin software that it installs in addition to

> **Use several AirPort Expresses for a network that reaches every nook of your house.**

the simple AirPort Express Assistant, however, is above reproach. It keys into a wonderful new feature of the AirPort Express called Profiles, which gives you the ability to switch your network settings very simply between various networks. This works outstandingly well if you unplug one of the bits of your home network, such as your notebook machine, and take it with you on the road, as you can create a profile for your wanderings, then a profile for your normal configuration, and switch between the two easily and seamlessly.

Penetrating Concrete with Software

Back to my original problem. Facing the specter of running Cat 5 Ethernet throughout my home and through some cement walls, I decided to look into a special access-point mode called Wireless Distribution System (WDS) first. The idea behind WDS is simple enough: master base stations are connected to the internet via a router or switch, and relay base stations are connected to the master base station via the same 802.11 connection that the relays push out to clients. In essence, they are signal repeaters for the main base station.

You'll find the AirPort Express ID on the underside of the unit.

The key piece in all of this is that connectivity must be established at both ends of the wireless link. When you set up your master base stations, it's important to have the AirPort IDs of the other base stations you intend to use as part of your wireless mesh. Fortunately, Apple has decided that those ID numbers belong on the devices themselves, making them very easy to find, as part of a label on the underside of the brick. Adding a remote base station is as easy as typing in

the AirPort ID into the system, then configuring the AirPort Express to use WDS for the connection and to select the primary base station. The whole process of creating a wireless mesh took me 10 minutes, from out-of-box to "Wow, That Rocks!"

When Wires Beat Wireless

Apple's AirPort Extreme Base Stations first brought WDS to the consumer a year or so ago, allowing users to configure their AirPorts as signal relays and remote relays, making for networks expanded through wireless linkages. All is not sunshine and roses with WDS, however. There's a decent amount of packet loss between the farthest relay base station and the master base station.

Handling real-time events like streaming video or audio is pretty dismal from the front to the back of my house. Events like networking, however, are fairly smooth. Printing via the AirPort Express is even simpler, as it's all handled by the Rendezvous/Zeroconf networking and printing protocols. The AirPort handles the heavy lifting and the printer the light work. Printing, much like music, however, isn't exactly meant to be done from across the WDS part of the network. If you're planning a print station, plan to have it be part of the wired network.

Overall, these devices are little tiny wonders, serving as eye-catching conversation pieces, instead of the eyesore that loose, tangled cabling would be. Allowing me to control my stereo via my laptop is an interesting parlor trick, as is printing over this new wireless network. It's good to show people it can be done, but it needs some serious work to make these features viable in the long term.

In order for this to be more than just a parlor trick, Apple has to do one of two things: either streamline the overhead in the printing transaction, or advise the user that printing over the network can be glacially slow. What pleases me most about the AirPort Express is the connectivity it provides my house, from end to end, without anything so much as a bit of radio, and that makes it worth every penny.

Tom Bridge is a writer and technologist living in northern Virginia.

Illustrations by Damien Scogin

smoothed his suit. His dark wrinkled face, red as a beet with mountain sunburn, gleamed in the candlelight like rich wood. He reminded Kaye of a toy troll she had loved as a child. From a box concealed under the table he brought out a small crystal glass, intricately cut and beveled. He took a beautiful silver-chased ibex horn and walked to a large amphora propped in a wooden crate in the near corner, behind the table. The amphora, recently pulled from the earth of his own small vineyard outside Tbilisi, was filled with some immense quantity of wine. He lifted a ladle from the amphora's mouth and poured it slowly into the horn, then again, and again, seven times, until the horn was full. He

READING eBOOKS ON A PALM HANDHELD

Discover the pleasures of reading by backlight.
By Mark Frauenfelder

I've tried using a few different dedicated eBook readers. They suck; they're much worse than paper books. But I do like using my Palm OS handheld as an eBook reader, especially at night in bed with the backlight on. Last year I bought a Sony CLIE T615C with a color 320x320 screen for about $75 used on eBay. I see they're going for as little as $50 on eBay now, a great deal for a 16MB device.

The screen is about 2.5x2.5 inches and it's at least as legible as a computer screen, if not more. The pixels are very small and the characters are very sharp. This high resolution is key for reading — the kind of screen that comes with the

Treo 600, for example, is no good for long texts (although I have a friend who keeps eBooks on his Treo and swears by it because it gives him something to read when he is in line or waiting for an appointment). Any Palm device will work, but standard low resolution (160x160) makes it more difficult to read. The Sonys and the Palm Tungsten have that satisfying high resolution (320x320). Recently, I picked up a Tapwave Zodiac, a combination PDA/handheld gaming unit with a 480x320 display. It's even better than the CLIE for read-

Books on handheld devices are actually easier to read than their dead-tree counterparts.

ing eBooks. Because the Zodiac was introduced only recently, you won't find many bargains for them on eBay. Expect to pay about $200 for a low-end version on eBay, or around $275 retail.

From the Web to the Palm in Almost One Easy Step

What do I read on my handheld? Articles and books. Typically, I'll cut and paste articles from websites into a text file. Then, once a week or so, I'll convert this text file into a Palm-readable document. The best program I've found for this task is PorDiBle (*pordible.victoly.com*), a free text-to-PDB converter application for OS X. I just drag the text file onto the PorDiBle icon and it creates a PDB file, which I double-click to load into the HotSync installer that comes with the Palm Desktop software. Another method to convert text files is to use the platform-independent web-based converter at *www.iconv.com/makedoc.htm*. It's even more convenient than PorDiBle, but you need to be online to use it.

Where to Find eBooks

As for books, I've read a few dozen on my PDA and have come to resent having to use real books, which now seem too heavy to have to prop up.

I get the books from two sources: Project Gutenberg (*gutenberg.net*) and eReader (*ereader. com*). Project Gutenberg has thousands of free, public-domain books. Thanks to the efforts of volunteers who scan books and run the files through optical, character-recognition software, I've downloaded and read *Anna Karenina, Huckleberry Finn, Sister Carrie, The Count of Monte Cristo, The Autobiography of Buffalo Bill,* and *David Copperfield*. Gutenberg's texts are formatted at 80-characters wide, so I have to remember to copy the text of Gutenberg's books into a text editor such as BBEdit and remove the line breaks before I convert them to the Palm PDB format.

EReader.com sells books for Palm and Windows handhelds. It has lots of the books I want, like Steven Johnson's *Mind Wide Open* and Bill Bryson's *A Brief History of Nearly Everything.* The prices are good, too. *Mind Wide Open* costs $13.49 here. It's $17.50 on Amazon in paper. Best of all, there's no waiting for the book to show up in the mail — you get it the instant you pay for it.

To read the books and articles I download from the web, Gutenberg, and eReader, I use the free eReader application from *eReader.com*. It's rock solid and it allows bookmarking, searching, and note taking.

When I lived on a tiny island in the South Pacific last year, it had one bookstore, which was about as exciting as an airport paperback kiosk. I was grateful to have access to thousands of books and articles via my handheld.

Mark Frauenfelder is editor-in-chief of MAKE.

Watching Video on a Handheld

Here's an easy way to copy your DVDs onto a Palm handheld for mobile viewing.

When I got my Tapwave Zodiac multimedia handheld, it came pre-loaded with video trailers for *Shrek 2* and *King Arthur*. They looked great on the Zodiac's VGA half-screen color display, and the sound coming out of the tiny built-in speakers was surprisingly loud and clear. My two daughters, age seven and one, were fascinated by the two-minute video clips and watched them over and over using the included Kinoma player ($20, *www.kinoma.com*).

Eventually, they asked for more. I thought it might be fun to copy some clips from their favorite DVDs onto the device's 256MB flash memory card, so I hit Google in search of a way to rip DVDs and convert the video to a format. Four hours later, I resurfaced with a bunch of different ripping, resizing, and reformatting applications, which, when cobbled together, yielded a bloated 15-second movie file that played on my Zodiac. I proved to myself that it could be done, but it was an impractical solution at best.

I was about to give up, but I went to Google one last time and was rewarded with a free program called HandBrake (*handbrake.m0k.org*) that converts DVD movies to the MPEG-4 format. After slipping a DVD into my iBook, I selected a title I wanted to convert. The application gave me the options of specifying the target size and scale of the converted file. A few minutes later, the file was ready. I copied it over to my Zodiac, and lo and behold, it worked flawlessly on Kinoma player. Now I have a good excuse to buy a 512MB flash memory card. — MF

PAIRING A BLUETOOTH HEADSET WITH A MAC

Using a wireless headset with Apple's iChat AV isn't as easy as you might think. By Dori Smith

I once read a review of a bug zapper — a product that killed flying insects. The reviewer concluded that once you took into account the product's pros and cons, your best value for the dollar was to buy it and then give it to your next-door neighbor. In so doing, you'd end up with most of the pros and none of the cons. Using iChat AV with a Bluetooth-enabled headset has a lot in common with that product, including the way that both of them leave you complaining about bugs.

Nonetheless, getting a Bluetooth headset to work with iChat AV is a worthwhile and liberating endeavor. Here's how you do it, along with a number of gotchas and workarounds you should know

about to ensure a successful pairing between headset and computer.

What You'd Expect

Mac users expect that they can plug things in (or in this case, pair things up), and they'll just work. So you'd expect that a Bluetooth headset pairing would allow you to use your Mac and your headset to do things like voice recognition, listen to iTunes, and in general, use the audio input and output features of the headset to replace the audio input and

> Getting a Bluetooth headset to pair up with a Mac isn't exactly "plug-and-play."

output of the Mac. Unfortunately, it's not quite that simple.

The Installation Process

There are three separate downloads, all of which are required: Bluetooth Firmware Updater 1.0.2, Bluetooth Software 1.5, and iChat AV 2.1. The firmware updater has the most ominous warning message I've ever seen in an Apple product, with five separate warnings (as shown in Figure 1).

Figure 1: Apple's Bluetooth Firmware Updater

Even if you pay attention to all these warning messages, things can still go wrong. If you were an early adopter and bought the original Bluetooth adapter sold by Apple (the D-Link DWB-120M), you'll get an error message saying that your adapter isn't suitable and its firmware isn't updateable. (The Belkin F8T003 isn't updateable, either, but the current adapter Apple sells, the D-Link DBT-120, works fine.)

But if you do have a compatible adapter, even with all those warning messages, Apple missed one: Don't run the firmware updater with Bluetooth turned off. The updater won't be able to find your Bluetooth device, and it won't stop trying -- leaving you with only an option specifically warned against: canceling the update. Thankfully, it appeared that no harm was done to my test machine, and the updater ran just fine after I turned on Bluetooth.

If you've gone to Apple's Bluetooth page (*apple. com/bluetooth*) to download both the Bluetooth software and the firmware updater, you might think you have everything that's necessary. After all, the page says, "You can also use a Bluetooth headset to talk to your friends and colleagues during an iChat AV session." But the page neglects to mention that the version of iChat AV you probably have (v2.0) only mostly works with Bluetooth headsets.

Save yourself several headaches and gray hairs (it's too late for me) and download iChat AV 2.1 (*apple.com/ichat/download*). While the only feature Apple documents adding in 2.1 is the ability to video conference with AOL 5.5/Windows users, installing 2.1 fixed a number of hairy Bluetooth iChat bugs on my test system, including application freezes and an inability to turn off Bluetooth devices.

Getting Started

You might think that upon installation of those downloads, your system would sync up with the new software and you'd be ready to use your headset, but remember, this isn't plug-and-play. You have to go into your System Preferences and select the Bluetooth-enabled headset. Your Sound System Preferences and the iChat Preferences each have separate settings for sound input and output (see Figures 2 and 3).

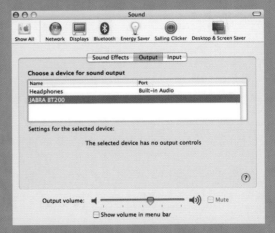

Figure 2: System Preferences > Sound pane

While this seems counterintuitive at first (two separate inputs and two separate outputs?), it starts to make sense shortly after you've tried using the headset for all system sounds. For instance, if your Mac hasn't made any sounds in a while, it drops the connection to your headset. If an application then beeps, the connection has to resume before the beep can be sent, causing a delay that makes you wonder just which recent action went with that beep. And listening to iTunes through the headset is near painful;

Photograph by Mark Frauenfelder

listeners unfavorably compared it to AM radio through a cheap speaker.

Figure 3: iChat AV > Preferences > Video pane

As for setting your System Preferences to use the headset for sound input, there's really not much point, as Apple documents fairly clearly that "Speech recognition is not a supported feature." The Speech System Preferences pane successfully recognizes the headset as a microphone and displays that it's hearing sounds, but you can't use it to enter speakable items. The day that we'll be able to wirelessly talk to our Macs is coming, but it's not here yet. Between the issues with system sounds, iTunes quality, and lack of speech recognition, there's no point in setting your Sound Preferences (neither input nor output) to use your Bluetooth headset.

Setting Things Up

The actual setup of a Bluetooth headset is fairly straightforward, although still somewhat more involved than plug-and-play:

1. Launch the Bluetooth Setup assistant.

2. Choose the new-to-Bluetooth 1.5 "Headset" radio button.

3. Set your headset to be discoverable, and wait for your Mac to find it.

4. At the prompt, enter the passkey associated with the headset (Hint: if you have the Jabra BT200, it's "0000").

5. Launch iChat AV.

6. Go to "iChat (Beta)" > "Preferences..." > "Video" (Because you'd expect to find the audio settings under the video preferences, right?).

7. Set the "Microphone" and "Sound Output" pop-up menus to your headset, as shown in Figure 3.

8. Start talking to your buddies.

Thankfully, all those steps only have to be done the first time; after that, when necessary, you'll simply be prompted to re-pair the device (as shown in Figure 4).

Figure 4: Pairing the headset

Don't believe that line about "Passkeys are only used once and do not need to be remembered." You'll need to repeat this step every time you turn the headset off (which includes recharging it) or go out of Bluetooth range and come back again. And even though your Mac knows that it's a headset and that you can't enter a passkey on a headset, it'll tell you, "The same passkey needs to be entered on both the computer and the remote Bluetooth device." So be sure to remember your passkey!

HARDWARE NEEDED:	SOFTWARE NEEDED:
A Mac running OS X 10.3.2 or higher	Bluetooth Firmware Updater 1.0.2
A Bluetooth module, either internal (supported by all) or external (only supported by some)	Bluetooth Software 1.5 iChat AV 2.1
A Bluetooth-enabled headset, such as the Jabra BT200	

iChatting with Bluetooth: Plug and Pray

Finally you've got everything set up just the way you want it, and you'll find that it works well, although not perfectly. If you've used iChat before, you'll find that the greatest new feature is being able to pace while chatting: no more having to talk directly into your iSight or PowerBook's microphone. And the combination of iChat, an iSight, and your Bluetooth headset is the virtual equivalent of VoIP calling.

I got mixed reports from the people I chatted with about the relative audio quality. While they all agreed that the headset was considerably better than my 15" PowerBook's built-in microphone, they split just about evenly on whether the headset was better or worse than the iSight's mic. The most common evaluation was that the two were fairly comparable in quality, but their tone was different, and different people preferred one over the other (sometimes strongly).

I was hoping that the headset would clear up what I consider to be iChat AV's greatest failing: the echo effect. It's distracting to hear everything I say repeated on the other end. The good news is that the headset does kill off the echo. The bad news: it kills it off for the person you're chatting with, not you. So you'll still hear an echo, but the person on the other end won't. Consequently, I found that I got the greatest enjoyment from the headset when I gave it to other people to use while I was chatting with them (hence the bug zapper analogy). The ideal situation would be if both parties used this set-up, because it would entirely eliminate echo from the conversation.

You'll also want to be careful about how you seat the headset in and around your ear — while it's supposed to fit everyone, nothing that's "one size fits all" ever quite does. Proper positioning of both the earbud and the mic improves the quality of both the sound input and output.

Final Thoughts

If it's important to you (as it is to me) to pace while you talk, you owe it to yourself to get a Bluetooth headset to use with iChat AV. If you don't currently have any audio input to your Mac and you already have Bluetooth, this is a simple way to be able to start audio chatting.

But beyond that, this technology is still not quite there yet. The big benefits I found were those available when I gave the headset to others to use instead of me: the end of the echo (on my end), and the ability to audio chat with people who previously had no access to sound inputs (while I had my internal PowerBook mic and iSight).

Eventually Apple will support features like speakable items and voice recognition. In the long run, we'll get functionality that lets our Macs, cell phones, and headsets interoperate, such that we can be listening to quality music on a headset until a phone call comes in. At that point, iTunes will pause, caller ID will show up on the Mac revealing who's calling, and we'll be able to take that call via the headset. We're close, but we're not quite there yet.

(Thanks to Tom, Matt, Al, Chuq, Steven, Eric, Lynn, Chuck, and Dan for help with the audio tests.)

Dori Smith is co-author of *Mac OS X Unwired* and *JavaScript for the WWW: Visual QuickStart Guide*.

A Bevy of Blueteeth

Before buying a Bluetooth headset, it's a good idea to go to a bricks and mortar store and try them out for fit and comfort. (Bring a box of alcohol wipes if you're concerned about germs.) Some of the models worth checking out:

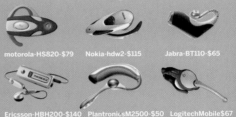

motorola-HS820-$79   Nokia-hdw2-$115   Jabra-BT110-$65

Ericsson-HBH200-$140   Plantronics-M2500-$50   LogitechMobile-$67

FUN iPOD TRICKS
Four ways to extend the usefulness of your digital music player. By Wei-Meng Lee

I'm constantly amazed by how versatile the iPod really is. It's more than just a music player; it's an information device. Not only can you use your iPod to play music from your favorite singer or band, you can use it to listen to radio recordings, "audio weblogs" (known as podcasts), and more. Here are some tips for getting the most out of your iPod, including how to manipulate the files stored there.

Tip #1 — Recording Internet Radio

You've seen many FM radio transmitters designed for the iPod, but you haven't seen (though you may have heard of) radio receivers for the iPod. For whatever reasons, you're unlikely to see FM radio receivers for your iPod anytime soon. So what do you do if you want to listen to radio broadcasts using your iPod?

Fortunately, internet radio broadcasting is making radio broadcasts accessible, especially if you want to tune in overseas. To listen to radio on your iPod, you need to save the radio broadcast on your Mac and then copy it onto your iPod.

My favorite tool for this is Oleg Kibirev's Radio-Recorder (*u1.netgate.net/~snowcat/RadioRecorder. html*), a free application released under the GNU General Public License, Version 2.

Using the RadioRecorder is straightforward: simply type the URL of the broadcasting station and you're ready to record. The radio program is recorded as an MP3 file, and MP3s are relatively large, so you need to be sure you have sufficient disk space on your Mac before you do the actual recording. From my experience, one minute of recording takes up approximately 1MB of disk space, so budget for it.

The RadioRecorder also allows you to program it to record at a specific time (see Figure 1). One thing — you have to keep the application open or it won't record. It can split the songs broadcasted into different files, provided the radio stations send the titles of the songs they play.

Figure 1. Using the RadioRecorder

Best of all, the RadioRecorder automatically links with iTunes so that the radio recordings can be copied to your iPod the next time you connect your iPod to your Mac (see Figure 2).

Figure 2. Viewing the recorded radio broadcast in iTunes

Tip #2 — Podcasting

Podcasting is a new term associated with weblogs. Increasingly, media files besides the usual text and graphics are found in weblogs. RSS

2.0 supports a new feature known as enclosure, which is a URL pointing to media files mentioned in an RSS feed.

Podcasting is the aggregation of discrete, downloadable media files. While the term podcasting suggests an association with Apple's iPod, it is important to point out that podcasting is not limited to use with the iPod. For example, you can use Windows Media Player to listen to a podcast.

iPodder (*ipodder.sourceforge.net*) is a small application that runs on both Mac and Windows. It periodically downloads audio files from the internet and copies them to iTunes so that they can be copied to your iPod. You can download other podcasting clients from Adam Curry's *ipodder.org*. iPodderX is a popular Mac client.

Using iPodder, you can subscribe to several news feeds containing media files (see Figure 3).

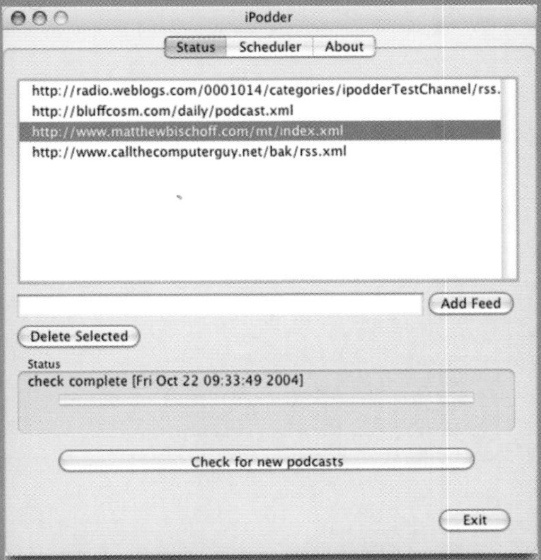

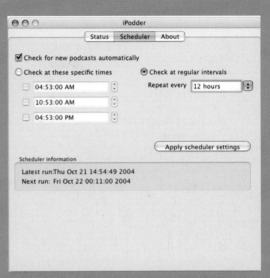

Figure 4. Configuring iPodder to download new podcasts at regular time intervals

Figure 3. Using iPodder

It's also quite easy to configure iPodder to check for any new podcasts at regular intervals (see Figure 4).

Once the podcasts are downloaded, you can find them in iTunes (see Figure 5). And the next time you connect your iPod to your computer, these podcasts will be copied onto your iPod if you have set up iTunes to sync with your iPod.

You can find a bunch of podcast feeds to get you started at *www.ipodder.org*. You'll have gigs of podcasts in no time.

Tip #3 — Working with Music Files on Your iPod

By default, iTunes will automatically update all songs and playlists in your iTunes Library. This is evident from the grayed-out song lists in iTunes.

There are times when you may want to free up space on your iPod. One way to delete unwanted songs on the iPod is to delete songs in the iTunes Library and synchronize your iPod with iTunes again. However, you may want to keep the songs on your Mac and delete them only from the iPod.

One way to solve this problem is to change the sync option on your iPod from automatic to manual. Right-click on your iPod's name in iTunes and select iPod Options (see Figure 5).

Figure 5. Configuring iPod's options

Select the "Manually manage songs and playlists" option and click OK (see Figure 6).

You should now notice that your iPod playlist in iTunes is selectable. Select the song(s) you want to delete and press the Delete key on your keyboard. This will remove the song(s) from your iPod.

Figure 6. Changing the iPod's update option

Tip #4 — Locating and Copying Music Out of Your iPod

Once your songs are copied to your iPod, how do you copy them out? To prevent the theft of music, Apple has hidden the music files on your iPod by assigning an "invisible" flag to each of the files and the folders that contain them. To extract them, you can use disk tools like ResEdit to manually copy the files onto your Mac. But this is not for the faint-hearted, because the improper

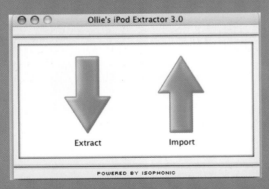

Figure 7. Using Ollie's iPod Extractor 3.0

use of ResEdit can corrupt the files you're work-ing on if you don't know what you're doing. For the rest of us, we can simply rely on third-party tools to do the song extraction.

Ollie's iPod Extractor 3.0 (*www.isophonic.net/*

applications) is one such song extractor for the iPod. You can download the tool and then use it to extract and import songs from/to your iPod (see Figure 7).

Here's how to use the program to extract songs from your iPod. Click on the Extract icon and a dialog box will prompt you to select your iPod (see Figure 8). Select your iPod name and click Open.

Figure 8. Selecting the iPod to extract songs using Ollie's iPod Extractor 3.0

Figure 9. Examining the saved songs

Then select a destination folder in which you want to save the extracted songs, and click Open.

The extracted songs will be stored in a folder named Music (see Figure 9). The songs are stored in multiple sub-folders under a folder named Music. Congratulations — your songs have been liberated!

Wei-Meng Lee founded Developer Learning Solutions and is the author of O'Reilly's *Windows XP Unwired*.

URBAN CAMOUFLAGE

With the right accessories, your vehicle can always be on "official business." By Todd Lappin

It started as a scam to find on-street parking. One day, I had a social-engineering epiphany — if I decorated my car to make it look like a commercial vehicle, I'd be able to park in yellow-curb loading zones without getting tickets from the overzealous parking control officers who regularly swarmed my neighborhood.

After a trip to an art-supply store to buy some vinyl lettering, a fake company name was created, decals were applied, and indeed, no parking tickets were received.

That was 18 years ago. Since then, all my vehicles have been decked out in corporate camouflage, even as my needs have evolved. In addition to basic parking acquisition, my current car, a 1999 Jeep Cherokee I ordered new from the factory in fleet-service white, has been config-

ured for urban vandalism deterrence, high-alpine winter driving, assisting stranded motorists, and infiltrating the abandoned military bases where I like to take photographs.

In these pages, I'll reveal the sources and methods I employed to create an effective vehicular disguise. With this covert knowledge, however, comes great responsibility. I don't condone using any of this for nefarious purposes. But like the old Hollywood cop-show cliché about the diaper-service delivery van that functions as a stake-out surveillance post, just remember — the company vehicle you see parked on your street or bearing down in your rear-view mirror may not be quite what it seems.

With a "company" vehicle, you'll enjoy special benefits and respectful admirers.

Push Bumper:

This is the same push bumper found on many police cars and highway service vehicles. Manufactured by Setina (*www.setina.com*), it's rubberized, so it's ideal for gently pushing stalled vehicles and protecting the front end during parallel parking maneuvers.

Police-Style Spotlight:

Manufactured by Unity (*www.unityusa.com*), my police-style spotlight looks official, rotates 360 degrees, and emits a retina-burning beam. It's legal in most states, and when used with discretion, it's ideal for rendering roadside assistance, finding street addresses, and scaring the bejesus out of teenagers parked on Lover's Lane. Mounting the spotlight requires significant drilling.

Funeral Sign

If used sparingly, a funeral visor sign can be very effective in eliciting sympathy from motorists and parking authorities. I had my sign laminated and Velcro-backed to preserve its fresh appearance.

Emergency Supplies

I carry these tools to get myself — and other hapless souls — unstuck: a 10,000-pound nylon tow strap, jumper cables, wrenches and screwdrivers, two Maglite flashlights, a handheld CB radio, duct tape, cable ties, a whistle, leather gloves, and a first-aid kit.

Fire Extinguisher:

My first car — a battered Dodge Monaco — burned itself to a hollow crisp alongside a Rhode Island interstate. Here's what I learned: car fires usually start small, but without a fire extinguisher, the flames quickly grow big. A 2.5LB extinguisher will do the trick ... don't leave home without it.

The Urban Camouflage Vehicle Makeover

Amber Hazard Flashers:

Mounted inside the vehicle for stealth purposes, these amber flashers light up like a Christmas tree at the flick of a switch. They're useful for traffic diversion and communication with freeway tailgaters. I bought mine from AW Direct (*www.awdirect. com*), my favorite catalog for tow-truck equipment.

Hazard Striping:

Nothing says "Keep Back" more subliminally than yellow-and-black caution stripes. I hired a local body shop to apply mine using automotive-grade paint, but vinyl tape is a cheaper alternative. Seton (*www.seton.com*) sells durable OSHA Safety Tape in a variety of widths and color combinations.

D-Ring Shackle:

This handy little shackle from Warn Industries (*www.gowarn.com*) mounts in a standard trailer hitch. I use it as an anchor point when extracting vehicles stuck in heavy snow, but it also provides a rugged impact point for parallel parking.

Fleet Vehicle Markings:

A cumbersome fleet number applied to each corner of the vehicle conveys the impersonal sprawl of a big corporation. Most office supply stores sell vinyl letters and numbers, in a variety of sizes, fonts, and colors.

E54130

E54130

Illustrations by Damien Scogin

SMOKEMOBILE
WE'RE PARKED OUTSIDE.™

"YOU'VE BEEN SERVED"
B.S.
BUSINESS SERVICES INC.
SINCE 1969

"SPEEDY"
DELIVERY

Ball 'n' Swoosh
WE'RE EVERYWHERE

Company Logos:

When concocting a company name, I wanted something that would sound authoritative but ambiguous. The logo I chose formerly belonged to a 1950s nuclear energy mutual fund. I had the vinyl decals custom-cut at Sign-A-Rama (*www.signarama.com*), a national chain, for about $100.

OMNITECH
Technology is Everywhere

NOT AN UNDERCOVER SURVEILLANCE VEHICLE INC.

Dynamic International Coiffure Supply

LINES
EFFICIENT. AUTHORITATIVE. CORPORATE-LOOKING.

Fake logos by Jorge Colombo, Kirk von Rohr, and David Albertson

Todd Lappin is a senior editor at *Business 2.0* magazine in San Francisco.

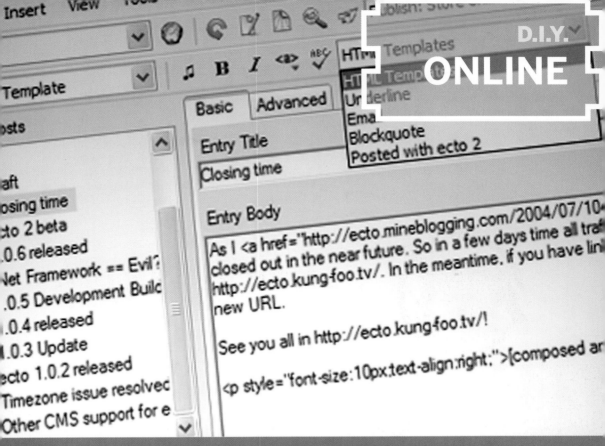

USING ECTO FOR ALMOST AUTOMATIC BLOGGING

An easy-to-use application to manage routine and time-consuming weblog chores.
By Mark Frauenfelder

To be a blogger is to know the drudgery of entering countless HTML tags by hand, as well as resizing and uploading images. The two most popular blogging applications, Blogger (*blogger.com*) and Movable Type (*movabletype.org*) only go so far in automating the grunt work that goes into posting an entry to your weblog.

I use Movable Type to maintain the blog I co-edit, *boingboing.net*. There are many wonderful things about the application, including its powerful archiving, search, and discussion features, but I found it to be lacking in the area I was most interested in: posting entries. I hated having to type <a href="http://example.com">Link</a> for every post I wrote, and I especially hated having to open up Adobe Photoshop to resize photographs that I wanted to include in an entry. I would often make a typo in an HTML tag, and the entire page would render in italics or the color red.

A couple of weeks after I started using Movable Type, I read another blogger's wild praise for an application with the funny-sounding name of Ecto. This program, enthused the blogger, automated all the

Ecto's powerful blogging features make up for Movable Type's weak editing tools.

repetitive chores that are a part of blogging. So I downloaded the two-week free trial of Ecto from *ecto.kung-foo.tv,* and within a few minutes, I, too, was madly in love with the $17.95 application. (Ecto also works with Blogger, but doesn't offer image resizing and uploading like it does with Movable Type, making it not very useful as a Blogger facilitator.)

Setting up Ecto is quite simple. Just open Accounts from the Window menu, and fill out a short form with information about where your weblog resides, along with your Movable Type username and password. I had no trouble recalling the information I needed to enter here. (If you've forgotten your Movable Type password, you can get it emailed to you from your MT Main Menu page, typically found at *www.yourblog.com/ cgi-bin/mt/mt.cgi,* where *www.yourblog.com* is the address of your weblog.)

To create a blog entry, just click New and start typing. The HTML menu, which contains a bunch of commonly used HTML strings (plus the capability to assign your own keyboard shortcuts to your favorite tags), makes entry-writing a breeze. It also reduces the possibility of typos that could mangle your website. I like being able to copy the URL from a website I am writing about, go back to Ecto, highlight my blog entry, and select "URL with clipboard" from the HTML menu. This idiot-proof action creates a properly formed hypertext link. I've also set up my own keyboard shortcuts for making text red, formatting text as a block-quote, and putting a strikeout line through text.

If you're obsessed with the word count of your blog entry, you can call up a Statistics window from the Draft menu that gives you the number of paragraphs, lines, and words in your entry. The feature counts actual words, not any HTML tags in the copy. I find all these features so useful that I often use Ecto as a word processor for short news stories I write for online magazines.

Ecto uses Mac OS X's built-in spellchecker to catch mispelled words on the fly. There's no the-saurus, but you can download a free one at *www. nisus.com/Thesaurus/* that does the trick.

As I hinted above, Ecto really shines when it comes to editing and uploading images. To use this feature, all I have to do is drag an image from a website or my desktop directly into the Ecto window. The application will resize and align the image according to my pre-specified format. (I usually choose "left alignment relative to text" because I like text to appear on the right side of my entries.) To edit these specifications, I click on the Image link and an image-editing window pops up. Here, I can add a border, turn the image into an enlargeable thumbnail, change the size, change the degree of compression, and so on. Once I have the image to my liking, I click the Apply button, and in a few seconds, the format-ted chunk of code for the image is automatically changed in my blog entry. There's no need to FTP the image into a folder; Ecto does that for me. Simple!

Ecto has a lot of other bells and whistles that make it easy to add stuff to your blog entries that would otherwise be a boring chore. A recently added feature, the Amazon Tool, is a nice way to add links to books and other products from *amazon. com* to your blog entries. Here's how it works: highlight a word or two in your blog entry, and then select Create Link > Amazon... from the menu. The Amazon Tool window (as shown) will pop up. Select a product category from the drop-down menu and click on Search. Ecto will return the top ten results, with thumbnail images of the product. If you click on the Options button, you can enter your Amazon Associate ID (if you have one) so that you can earn a little money should someone buy the product after reading about it on your blog. Now you can double-click on any of the products in the Amazon Tool window, and a link to the product will be added to your blog entry.

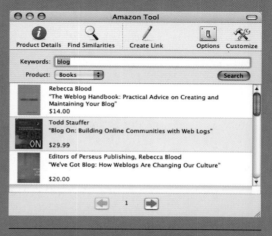

Mark Frauenfelder is editor-in-chief of MAKE.

アレックのバーチャルドメイン・ホスティングサービス

ちょ～グッドなインターネット総合サービス

Gメール

自社ドメインとメールアドレスで会社を効果的にアピール!!

TEN COOL GMAIL HACKS

With Gmail, Google has loosed upon the web another monstrously useful service.
By Geoffrey Litwack

Gmail is Godzilla; Hotmail is Tokyo. So what's next? Here's a sampling of some existing hacks, arrayed in ascending order of challenge.

Gmailit Bookmarklet
sippey.typepad.com/filtered/2004/06/
gmailto_bookmar.html
This JavaScript bookmarklet enables you to send the page you're viewing to someone via Gmail, along with any text you might have selected in the body of the message.

Gmail Icon Generator
www.nhacks.com/gmail/index.php
This simple form creates a beautiful icon of your Gmail address that you can display on a web page

or in a signature to avoid email-harvesting spam-bots — at least until they grow eyes with optical character recognition.

makezine@Gmail.com

Firefox Gmail Notifier
weblogs.mozillazine.org/doron/
archives/005836.html
This Gmail notifier gives you a toolbar icon in your Firefox browser that displays how many unread messages are sitting in your account. It takes one click to install, and works across all platforms. Not using Firefox? Try Google's own

notifier for Windows (*toolbar.google.com/ gmail-helper/*) or gCount, a menu bar and dock notifier for Mac OS X (*www.ocf.berkeley.edu/ ~natan/gcount/*).

Gmailto for Mac OS X
gu.st/code/Gmailto/
This clever little hacklet works with OS X's Mail application. When you click on a mailto: link that appears in your web browser, it intercepts it and opens a new blank message in your Gmail account. The same thing can be accomplished for Windows by selecting an option in Google's notifier preferences.

Mark Lyon's Gmail Loader
www.marklyon.org/gmail/default.htm
If you plan on using Gmail as your primary email service, you'll need to come up with a way to get all your old mail in there. Enter Gmail Loader, a Python script (an executable is available for Windows) that works by forwarding all your old email to Gmail. Until Google finally comes up with a built-in Import button, Gmail Loader is the next best thing.

GetMail for Hotmail
www.e-eeasy.com/getmail.aspx
Ready to bail out of Hotmail? GetMail gives you the capability to forward all of your mail from your Hotmail account to any other account, including a Gmail account. One of the virtues of this program is that if, like me, you have a Hotmail account you haven't checked in a while, you can forward the mail and Gmail's superior spam filtering algorithm will sort the cream from the cruft. (Lame spam filtering is one reason people don't like Hotmail in the first place.) For the time being, it only works under Windows, so if you're a Mac or Linux user, you might want to bite the bullet and use a friend's machine for this one-time task.

Gmail-mobile
sourceforge.net/projects/gmail-mobile/
If you love Gmail so much that you want to take it with you wherever you go, Gmail-mobile will do the trick. Taking the form of a PHP application, Gmail-mobile installs on a web server and gives you access to your Gmail account from any WAP-enabled phone. It allows you to read your mail, compose messages, access your labels, and more. Alternatively, if you're willing to trust an outside party with your password, you can use *gmailwireless.com* and spare yourself the installation process.

Gmail Backup
ilia.ws/archives/15_Gmail_as_an_online_ backup_system.html
The first thing many people think of when they get a Gmail account is how they can use it for online storage. This PHP utility wraps your Gmail account so it appears as storage to your file system — accomplishing the same thing as emailing attachments to yourself, but with more panache. It's unclear if this violates the terms of service, but Google seems to be tolerant of such innovations.

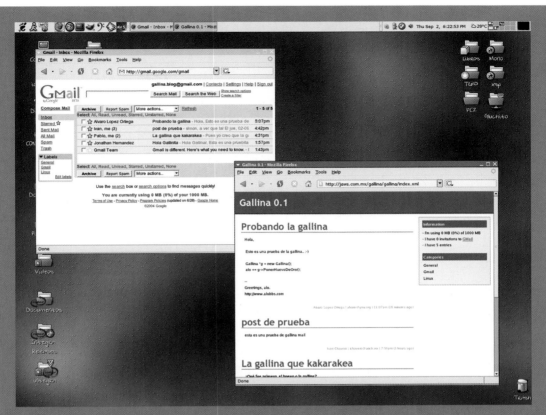

Gallina

ion.gluch.org.mx/files/Hacks/gallina/

Gallina is a simple blogging system you install on your web server that uses Gmail as a database. In order to post to your blog, all you do is mark a message in your account with a star. While it won't challenge Movable Type for weblog supremacy any time soon, it does support JPG and PNG attachments, and more features are on the way.

New Gmail Features

There are now fewer reasons than ever for not switching to Gmail. In November 2004, Google announced several new features for Gmail, the most important of which include POP access, so you can download your Gmail on any mail application and read it offline, and mail forwarding, so you can redirect your Gmail to another email address.

Gmail Wiki

www.gmailwiki.com/

Everything you could possibly want to know about Gmail crackles in the milk of this comprehensive wiki: tips, tricks, links, utilities, and more. If it's discussion you're after, try *gmailforums.com*, which is just what it sounds like.

Not satisfied? Make your own!

There's more where this came from. For serious hackers who want to roll their own Gmail services, Perl, PHP, and Python interfaces are in development. Check out Mail-Webmail-Gmail for Perl (*search.cpan.org/dist/Mail-Webmail-Gmail/*) or libgmail for Python (*libgmail.sourceforge.net/*). If you're looking for something even more powerful, GMailer, a PHP library (*gmail-lite.sourceforge.net/*) might do the trick for you. Because the Gmail service itself is ever-changing, these three are themselves undergoing rapid development.

Geoffrey Litwack lives at *litwack.org*.

TWO HANDY EXCEL HACKS
Calculating on the quick, plus fast formatting of imported dates.

Calculating a Column

Excel provides a bunch of nifty calculation tools that work on any group of number-holding cells that has been selected. After making a selection, the Status bar displays any one of the following results:

Average. The average of all the selected numbers or dates.

Count. The number of selected cells (including any cells with text in them).

Count Nums. The number of selected cells that contain numbers or dates.

Min. The selected number or date with the smallest value (for dates this means the earliest date).

Max. The selected number or date with the largest value (for dates this means the latest date).

Sum. The sum of all selected numbers.

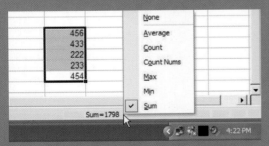

To choose one of these options, select all the cells to be included in the calculation, right-click anywhere on the Status bar, and choose from the menu that appears. The default option is Sum, which adds together all the selected cells. You'll see the calculated value displayed on the Status bar.

Most of the Status bar calculations won't work properly if you select both date and numeric information. For example, when attempting to add up a list of numbers and dates, the value will be computed using both the date values — which are calculated using a special set of rules — and the ordinary numbers, and the result will be displayed using the formatting of the first selected cell. That adds up, alas, to a number that doesn't really mean anything.

—*Matthew MacDonald*

Convert Dates to Excel-Formatted Dates

Dates imported from other programs frequently cause problems in Excel. Many people manually retype them, but there are easier ways to solve the problem.

The figure below shows a date format you might encounter after importing (column A).

As the figure shows, the formulas in column B convert the data in column A to three results in column C, all of which follow the U.S. date format of mm/dd/yy.

	A	B	C
	Old Date	Formula Used	Formula Result
2	112303	=VALUE(LEFT(A2,2)&"/"&MID(A2,3,2)&"/"&RIGHT(A2,2))	11/23/03
3	031123	=VALUE(MID(A3,3,2)&"/"&RIGHT(A3,2)&"/"&LEFT(A3,2))	11/23/03
4	231103	=VALUE(MID(A4,3,2)&"/"&LEFT(A4,2)&"/"&RIGHT(A4,2))	11/23/03
5			

Date formats converted to valid dates (U.S. format).

To convert to the European date format, simply swap the "MID," "LEFT," and "RIGHT" values so that the day, rather than month, appears first.

The next figure shows the same approach at work, except that the cells in column C were formatted with the European date format of dd/mm/yy.

	A	B	C
1	Old Date	Formula Used	Formula Result
2	112303	=VALUE(MID(A2,3,2)&"/"&LEFT(A2,2)&"/"&RIGHT(A2,2))	23/11/2003
3	031123	=VALUE(RIGHT(A3,2)&"/"&MID(A3,3,2)&"/"&LEFT(A3,2))	23/11/2003
4	231103	=VALUE(LEFT(A4,2)&"/"&MID(A4,3,2)&"/"&RIGHT(A4,2))	23/11/2003

Date formats converted to valid dates (European format).

Hopefully, these nifty formulas will take some of the stress out of working with imported dates.

—*David and Raina Hawley*

Excerpted from *Excel Hacks*, Copyright© 2004 O'Reilly Media.

SPEED UP YOUR TEXT ENTRY WITH TYPEIT4ME

If you're not an avid, constant user of TypeIt4Me, you're not really getting things done. By Mark Hurst

I'll go further and say you're hardly using your computer at all until you include TypeIt4Me in your daily computer usage.

TypeIt4Me (*typeit4me.com*) is a Mac-only shareware app. It costs $27. (For Windows users, ActiveWords — *www.activewords.com* — offers similar functionality, but I haven't used it.) TypeIt4Me works in both OS X and Classic mode, and across every application: BBEdit, Safari, Finder — even MS Office apps bend to its will.

Here's how it works: you define abbreviations and associated expansions in TypeIt4Me. When you type an abbreviation and then hit the trigger (usually the space bar, but it can be any punctuation mark, depending on your preferences), the abbreviation instantly gets replaced with the trigger. For example, if I type "cg" and hit the space bar, "cg" instantly turns into "Creative Good". The abbreviation-expansion function is all TypeIt4Me does, but that one function has enormous ramifications for every computer user on the planet.

Consider the Many Uses of TypeIt4Me

1. Corrects misspellings: "teh" becomes "the" and "taht" becomes "that". I can type a lot faster now, since I don't have to worry about common misspellings slowing me down. Over the years, I've added all of my most common misspellings, so now I can blaze on the keyboard and watch in amusement as TypeIt4Me instantly fixes the misspellings in my cursor's wake.

2. Expands my custom-defined shorthand: Some words are both common and lengthy. I use the word "experience" a lot, but in TypeIt4Me I just type "ex". Similarly, "ce" becomes "customer experience", "env" becomes "environment", and so on.

3. Types in long URLs: My email management report has a rather long URL: *www.goodexperience.com/reports/e-mail/email-report-goodexperience.pdf*. Rather than dig it up every time I need to paste it into a message, I just type "emu" and it pastes it in. Similarly, "geu" leads to *http://www.goodexperience.com*, "cgu" leads to *http://www.creativegood.com*, "tbu" turns into *http://www.thisisbroken.com*, etc.

4. Types in HTML phrases: I've defined "ahr" to yield <a href=""></a>. Whether I'm in BBEdit or in a TypePad form within a web browser, I can get these key HTML strings out quickly and error-free.

5. Manages passwords: My *wsj.com* password is stored as "wpw"; my *half.com* password is stored as "hpw"; you get the idea. This way, as I define the abbreviations for each password, all I have to do is remember the abbreviation — much easier than keeping track of a million different passwords.

6. Types short phrases: This is great in email. I've set it up so that "tf" becomes "thanks for"; "tfy" becomes "thanks for your"; "tvmfy" becomes "thanks very much for your"; and so on. You can be as polite as you want and optimally efficient at the same time.

7. Types long messages with multiple paragraphs: For those messages that I send to multiple people at different times, I write it once, define a TypeIt4Me abbreviation, then have it available for expansion any time. This works great when you

Cn yu rd ts?

Hendrik Hertzberg, senior editor of *The New Yorker*, is a fan of TypeIt4Me. He wrote: "I've discovered that this program is absolutely great as far as writing is concerned. Having built my data file one word at a time, I can, for the first time, write as fast as I can think. Or, to type those two sentences with expansion turned off: iv dscvd ta th prg s absl gr afa wrig s ksnd. Vg blt my data file one word at a ti, i c f t first ti wri as fast as i c tq."

email the same (or similar) message to people on occasion.

The key to TypeIt4Me is to start slow. Define a few abbreviation-expansion pairs each day, and see what "sticks." Which ones do you naturally remember? Which ones do you use a lot? It takes some time to get really effective with TypeIt4Me, but like any sound investment, the returns compound over time. I use most of the expansions every month, whether through a misspelling, a URL, a password, or for any other reason. My typing is fast.

But here's the important thing: I still add new expansions almost every day. I am determined to continue getting faster, more accurate, and more efficient in my bit-creation at every opportunity. TypeIt4Me isn't shareware that you install, define a few things in, and then call it a day. No. TypeIt4Me is a bit-lever — one essential component of bit literacy — and as such it requires an ongoing commitment toward mastery. Efficiency isn't something you accomplish in a day; it's something you grow into. It's a way of life.

Finally, a word of warning: if you use TypeIt4Me diligently for a few weeks and begin to realize its benefits in your efficiency, you will NEVER — read me, now — you will NEVER want to go back to a machine that doesn't run it. You will curse every Internet cafe PC that stupidly requires you to type every character; you will mutter under your breath on your friends' machines; you will be spoiled for life. But you will have seen the light. Isn't that worth it?

Mark Hurst is the founder of the media company Good Experience, Inc. (*www.goodexperience.com*).

A MAKER STORY

Salad-Bowl Hacking

Pizza Huts in China have a rule: only one trip to the salad bar. Naturally, customers heap as many items as they can into the small bowls. But some Pizza Hut regulars have turned salad stacking into a science, creating pillars of vegetables that dwarf the bowls that support them. Here are some images from a salad-bowl hacking manual written by a 27-year-old sofware engineer in China named Shen Hongrui. Download the PDF document (in Chinese) at *www.tinyurl.com/66vsn*.

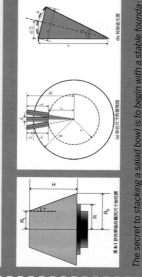

The secret to stacking a salad bowl is to begin with a stable foundation on which to construct a veritable tower of herbivorous delight.

Think of cucumber slices and pineapple chunks as bricks, and salad dressing as mortar.

To eat your creation, reverse the stacking procedure, substituting your mouth for the salad bar.

TINY PC TOTE

Make rubber tie-down handles for a Small Form Factor PC. By Marc H. Nathan

Small Form Factor (also known as Mini-ITX) computers religiously follow the mantra of all electronics: Smaller is Better. You might be thinking that a miniature full featured computer that has an all-in-one design is called a laptop — but that would miss the point of these well engineered specialty cases. They are technologically equal and sometimes even better than their full tower brethren, but these no-bigger-than-a-breadbox PCs are designed not only to free up precious desktop real estate, but to look good in the process.

The form factor has caused a bit of a renaissance in the DIY computer crowd who needed something more than a new chipset or hard drive interface to stay interested. This type of project is enormously fun as far as building computers

go, with all of the tight spaces and cable origami that comes with jamming full-size components into a half-size box. Recently, I was looking for my next case to turn into a PVR, when I found myself extolling the virtues of these little guys to the gathering crowd at Fry's. When I had finished evangelizing and came up for breath, one guy decided that it would be the perfect Linux starter computer and another person bought two to start his own cluster family. Aside from their obvious street cred in the mod scene and LAN party masses, SFF cases actually make decent desktop replacements for the buttoned down 9-to-5 Word and IE set — like mine does here. It rarely fails to bring

These rubber straps serve several purposes: handle, cable holder, and desktop protector.

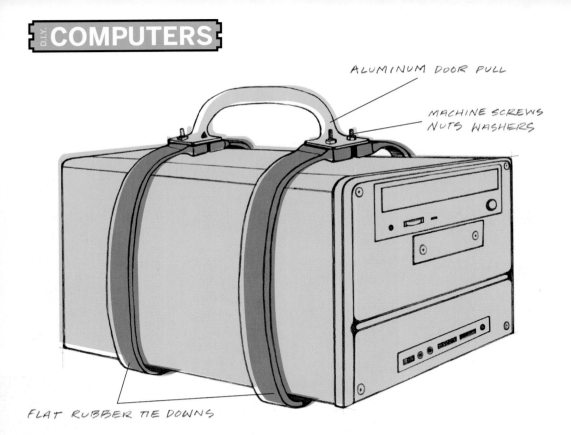

ALUMINUM DOOR PULL

MACHINE SCREWS
NUTS WASHERS

FLAT RUBBER TIE DOWNS

PARTS LIST:
2 Flat rubber tie-downs,
    31" each ($2 - $5)
1 Aluminum door pull,
    6" ($2 - $3)
4 Machine screws,
    ⅛"-diameter, 1"-long
4 Nuts, ⅛" ($2 - $3 for
    an assortment)

4 Washers, ⅛"

OPTIONAL EQUIPMENT:
Dremel to cut screws
    flush with nuts
Rounded screw caps

narrowly avoided attempt to drill holes in the top of the thin-walled aluminum case, I came up with this quick and dirty solution. The 31" tie-downs are just long enough to go around the PC, but have enough slack for stuffing wrapped cables under the handle. One unintended, but beneficial, consequence is that the tie-downs act as rubber feet that won't scratch or mar your desk.

It's easy to make. First, remove the "S" shaped hooks from the tie-downs. On a flat surface, place the tie-downs parallel to each other, approximately 6" apart, or as far apart as the handle is long. Place washers on top of the holes in the tie downs. Put the screws in the holes so that the screw heads are facing the top. Fasten the washers, handle, and nut to the underside of ONE side only (either right or left) of each tie-down. Set the PC in the middle of the tie-downs and bend the handle-side of the tie-downs up to the top of the PC. Fasten the other side of the tie-downs to the handle. (Make sure that the screws point up.) Adjust as needed and season to taste.

a smirk and a knowing wink to those who know what it is and an astonished "What's That?!" to those who don't.

The only real issue I have with these boxes is that they're shaped exactly like a box. It became unwieldy to carry it back and forth under my arm since I usually had other accessories with me as I moved from office to home and back. Certainly there are SFF cases with plastic molded handles on top, but since I like to stack an external back-up hard drive on top, those boxes didn't have much appeal to me. There are also carrying bags and nylon strap configurations specifically designed for this sort of thing, but they were too expensive for the problem they solved and I wanted something I could leave on all the time. After a

Marc Nathan is an angel investor and technology enthusiast who lives with his wife and two bulldogs in Houston, Texas.

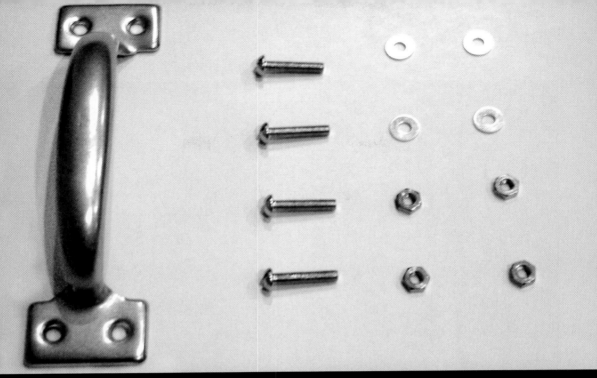

Once you collect the necessary hardware, it should only take a couple of minutes to make the handles.

To protect your case you might want to glue small pieces of rubber to the machine screw heads.

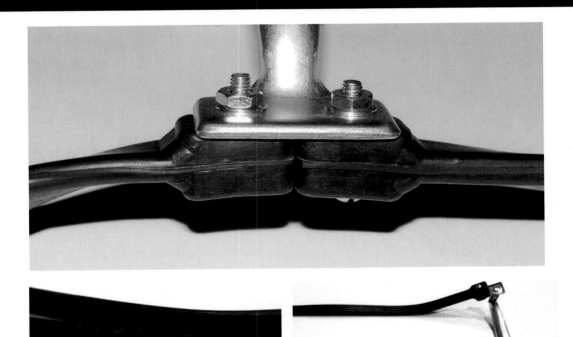

TAKING THE "VIDEO" OUT OF VIDEO GAME

Most people program video games. Niklas Roy built one, literally. The 30-year-old from Berlin, Germany, constructed a fully mechanized facsimile of one of the granddaddies of video games, Pong.

By Howard Wen

Photography courtesy of Niklas Roy

Roy's version, which he simply named *Pongmechanik*, is a sit-down, tabletop contraption of telephone relays, pulleys, string, and sheets of glass. It uses no microprocessors, semiconductors, or other electronic components. Even the sound of the square "ball" as it bounces across the playfield is produced through analog means: solenoids strike hollow, wooden sound blocks.

It took a full year for Roy to construct Pongmechanik. Having worked as a visual effects supervisor for movies, and currently studying at Berlin University of the Arts, his personal goal for the project was artistically philosophical.

In this interview, Roy explains the inspiration behind the old-school technology of Pongmechanik and why you probably shouldn't do what he did.

How did you get the idea to make a mechanical version of Pong?

As a visual effects supervisor, I have to create virtual worlds that look like reality. Creating digital copies of the world surrounding us is a fashionable thing. It is not only done in the film business — it is also done in the computer game industry.

The idea of Pongmechanik was to turn that thing around. I wanted to take a well-known virtual world — the tennis court of Pong — and put it into reality. For me, it was an artistic experiment. I wanted to find out if this can bring a "new quality" to the old game. This was the reason why I found it important to make an exact copy of it. I wanted to compare the systems — computer as a "box" that displays a virtual reality — with a three-dimensional machine, where you can see, hear, and feel all of the processes that happen.

That sounds like quite a mind-bender: Pongmechanik as a "real" interpretation of a game that is in itself an extremely simplified version of a "real" game — tennis. Which do you personally feel is the more real experience now: Pongmechanik or Pong? For example, is there something you see in Pong now that you hadn't noticed before?

For me, it is more real to play Pongmechanik than to play any other computer game. Also interesting is that it breaks often. My video game Pong at home is maybe over 20 years old, but it still works

> "The main difference between writing computer code and building a machine like this is that you have no 'copy-and-paste' and 'undo.' If you build a part that doesn't work, you have to build it again."

without any problems. If the video game breaks, I am sure I wouldn't have any idea how to repair it. But repairing Pongmechanik is usually no problem because you can see easily which mechanical part doesn't work anymore.

Another interesting point is that Pongmechanik makes mistakes. Sometimes it makes faults when counting the score; sometimes it doesn't return a ball even if it looks like you have hit it with your bat. There are usually electromechanical reasons for these problems. Some contacts don't work well enough, or the old telephone relays switch too slow, or whatever.

What were the challenges you had to deal with in building Pongmechanik?

Building a mechanical device that works fast and reliably was more complicated than I thought. It took me a second attempt to do it successfully. To be honest, the machine breaks quite often. If I would build another version, I would know what to change in the mechanics to make it more reliable. But I regard it as an art piece, and for me, it is much more important to know that it worked at least one time than always being able to play it.

How would you like people to regard Pongmechanik most? Is it more a gaming machine or a work of art as you've implied?

Pongmechanik appeals to a big range of people, and all of them like different things about it.

It doesn't matter if you like the machine because you are a computer freak or because you are interested in contemporary art. There are also some people who regard it as a strange piece of furniture.

Are you a programmer, or familiar with programming?

I am not a programmer, but I have written a lot of programs in higher languages.

Have you noticed any similarities between "programming" a mechanical system and writing software?

The logical problems are absolutely the same. In the mechanical and in the computer, there are equivalents of variables and if-thens. The main difference between writing computer code and building a machine like this is that you have no "copy-and-paste" and "undo." If you build a part that doesn't work, you have to build it again.

Is there a programming language you're familiar with that you would say compares closely to your experience in "programming" Pongmechanik?

I would compare it with ActionScript because of the events and because Pongmechanik consists of two parts: the mechanical device and the relay circuit. In Flash, you have the animation part and ActionScript.

Did you have to design any technology specifically for Pongmechanik?

The technologies are all old. The machine could have been built in the '30s, which is another interesting point of it. The only parts of the machine that they hadn't invented yet in the '30s were joysticks.

So why did you decide to use joysticks? Wouldn't rotary dial controllers have made more sense and fit with the "retro-futurism" you were going for? Would there have been a mechanical issue with using dials?

Rotary dials like in old telephones? I never thought about that, but this definitely would have been a good idea. The original Pong used paddles [controllers]. This is the only fault that I made when I wanted to build an exact copy of the game.

When I first saw your creation, it immediately brought to my mind the "mechanical computer" that Charles Babbage designed but never could build.

I don't know enough about the ideas of Babbage. But Konrad Zuse (who seems to be better known in Germany) designed the first fully programmable computer in the 1930s as a completely mechanical machine, which didn't need electricity to work. It just had a crank, which you had to move. It consisted of thousands of metal sheets which he had sewn out by hand with the help of friends. The computer never worked well. The problem is that the machine makes miscalculations depending on the outside temperature because the metal deforms.

I find it interesting that he used telephone relays for the calculation parts in his next machines but kept the design of the mechanical memory because it was more reliable, cheaper, and much smaller than relays.

Will you make another game with the technology you designed for Pongmechanik? I immediately wondered if a mechanical version of Breakout would be possible.

I thought about building a mechanical Pac-Man, but it would be complicated to keep it running.

I have made some other pieces. One is called *grafidemo*. It is the chassis of a [Commodore] CBM 3032 computer with a soldered wireframe model of a teapot inside. You can rotate the teapot on two axes by pushing keys on the keyboard.

What advice do you have for those who want to try building their own mechanized video game like you did?

Don't do it. It costs a lot of time and money, and in the end, you have a game that is slower than the original video game, breaks every second day, and needs a lot of space.

That's awfully discouraging! Pongmechanik is certainly a work of art, and good art can inspire its audience. What do you say to those who are inspired by your work?

Those who are inspired by my work should develop their own ideas showing how computers can be released out of their gray boxes, and how they can gain an emotional dimension. I would love to see computers like Pongmechanik that can do some-

> I wanted to take a well-known virtual world — the tennis court of Pong — and put it into reality.

thing else, but it would be boring to see hundreds of electromechanical Pongs.

Roy's game on the web: *pongmechanic.hasselt.org*

Howard Wen is a freelance writer who has written for *oreillynet.com*, *salon.com*, *playboy.com*, and Wired, among others.

SOLDERING & DESOLDERING

Step-by-step instructions for making (and unmaking) the perfect solder joint By Joe Grand

The two key parts of soldering are good heat distribution and cleanliness of the soldering surface and component. With practice, you'll become comfortable and experienced with the process.

In this primer, I'll explain how to solder a component onto a printed circuit board. I'll also provide desoldering tips and show you how to remove a surface-mount component from a printed circuit board using a Chip Quik kit. And I'll show you how to remove a component by removing the solder in a way that won't damage the components or the circuit board.

SOLDERING

SOLDERING A RESISTOR TO A CIRCUIT BOARD

BEFORE YOU START
Inspect the leads or pins for oxidation. If the metal surface is dull, sand with fine sandpaper until shiny. In addition, use the sandpaper to clean the oxidation and excess solder from the soldering iron tip to ensure maximum heat transfer.

This simple example shows the step-by-step process to solder a through-hole component to a printed circuit board (PCB). I used a piece of prototype PCB and a single resistor.

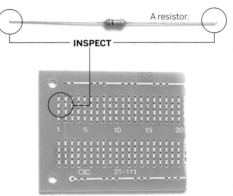

A resistor.

INSPECT

A printed circuit board.

> **DANGER** It's important to consider safety precautions. Improper handling of the soldering iron can lead to burns or other physical injuries. Wear safety goggles and other protective clothing when working with solder tools. With temperatures hovering around 700 degrees F, the tip of the soldering iron, molten solder, and flux can quickly sear through clothing and skin. Keep all soldering equipment away from flammable materials and objects. Be sure to turn off the iron when it is not in use and store it properly in its stand.

START »

1. Bend and insert the component leads into the desired holes on the printed circuit board (PCB). Flip the board to the other side. Slightly bend the lead you will be soldering to prevent the component from falling out when the board is turned upside down.

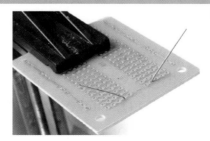

Resistor inserted into PCB.

Tools of the Trade

Soldering Iron: You could pay as little as $10 or as much as $1,000 for a soldering iron. I recommend a fine-tip, 700 degree F, 50W soldering stick iron. A good general-purpose iron for hardware hacking is the Weller W60P Controlled-Output Soldering Iron, which sells for under $70.

Solder: Should be thin gauge (0.032" or 0.025" diameter) 60/40 rosin core.

Desoldering Tool (AKA Solder Sucker): A manual vacuum device that pulls up hot solder, useful for removing components from circuit boards. I like the one RadioShack sells (#64-2098, $6.99).

IC Extraction Tool: Helps lift integrated circuits from the board during removal/desoldering.

Chip Quik SMD Removal Kit: Allows you to remove surface mount components quickly and easily. Visit *www.chipquik.com* for links to distributors. The kit is available for about $20.

Sandpaper: A very fine-grit sandpaper is useful for removing oxidation from component and circuit board surfaces.

Desoldering Braid: Woven metal material used to wick up melted solder.

Small, Flat-Tip Screwdriver: Comes in handy for removing some types of components.

Needle-Nose Pliers, Wire-Cutters, and Vise: These common tools will make your job easier.

---

2. To begin the actual soldering process, allow the tip of your iron to contact both the component lead and the pad on the circuit board for about one second before feeding solder to the connection. This will allow the surface to become hot enough for solder to flow smoothly.

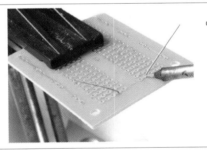

Heat the desired solder connection.

3. Next, apply solder sparingly and hold the iron in place until solder has evenly coated the surface. Ensure that the solder flows all around the two pieces (component lead and PCB pad) that you are fastening together. Do not put solder directly onto the hot iron tip before it has made contact with the lead or pad; doing so can cause a cold-solder joint (a common mistake that can prevent your hack from working properly). Soldering is a function of heat, and if the pieces are not heated uniformly, solder may not spread as desired. A cold-solder joint will loosen over time and can build up corrosion.

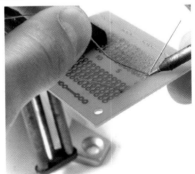

Apply heat and solder to the connection.

TIP: Every so often during any soldering process, use a wet sponge to lightly wipe the excess solder and burned flux from the tip of your soldering iron. This allows the tip to stay clean and heat properly. Proper maintenance of your soldering equipment will also increase its life span.

»

4. When it appears that the solder has flowed properly, remove the iron from the area and wait a few seconds for the solder to cool and harden. Do not attempt to move the component during this time. The solder joint should appear smooth and shiny, resembling the image at right. If your solder joint has a dull finish, reheat the connection and add more solder.

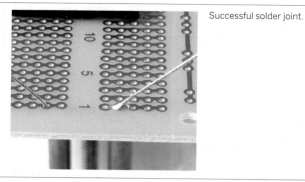

Successful solder joint.

5. Once the solder joint is in place, snip the lead to the desired length. Usually, you will simply cut the remaining portion of the lead that is not part of the actual solder joint. This prevents any risk of short circuits between leftover component leads on the board.

Snip off the remaining component lead.

6. Here's a completed soldering example.

Completed soldering example.

FINISH ☒

NOW GO DESOLDER 》

DESOLDERING

SMD REMOVAL WITH CHIP QUIK

Desoldering, or removing a soldered component from a circuit board, is typically trickier than soldering, because you can easily damage the device, the circuit board, or surrounding components. For surface mount devices (SMDs) with more than a few pins, the easiest method to remove the part is the Chip Quik SMD Removal Kit, as shown in the following step-by-step example.

Please read through this example completely before attempting SMD removal on an actual device. When removing the device, be careful not to scratch or damage any of the surrounding components or pull up any PCB traces.

START »

1. The first step is to assemble the syringe, which contains the no-clean flux. Simply insert the plunger into the syringe and push down to dispense the compound. The flux should be applied evenly across all the pins on the package you will be removing. Flux is a chemical compound used to assist in the soldering or removal of electronic components or other metals.

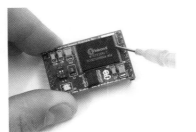

Apply flux to the leads.

Three Primary Functions of Flux:

» Cleans metal surfaces to assist the flow of filler metals (solder) over base metals (device pins).

» Assists with heat transfer from heat source (soldering iron) to metal surface (device pins).

» Helps in the removal of surface metal oxides (created by oxygen in the air when the metal reaches high temperatures).

Chip with flux applied.

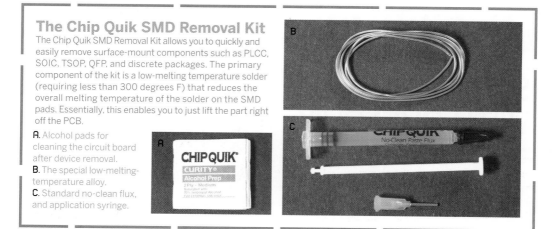

The Chip Quik SMD Removal Kit

The Chip Quik SMD Removal Kit allows you to quickly and easily remove surface-mount components such as PLCC, SOIC, TSOP, QFP, and discrete packages. The primary component of the kit is a low-melting temperature solder (requiring less than 300 degrees F) that reduces the overall melting temperature of the solder on the SMD pads. Essentially, this enables you to just lift the part right off the PCB.

A. Alcohol pads for cleaning the circuit board after device removal.
B. The special low-melting-temperature alloy.
C. Standard no-clean flux, and application syringe.

2. Once the flux is evenly spread over the pins of the target device, the next step is to apply the special Chip Quik alloy to the device. This step is just like soldering: apply heat to the pins of the device and the alloy at the same time. The alloy has a melting point of approximately 300 degrees F, which is quite low. You should not have to heat the alloy with the soldering iron for very long before it begins to melt. The molten alloy should flow around and under the device pins. Starting at one end of the device, simply heat and apply the alloy. Repeat for the other side(s) of the device. The flux will help ensure a nice flow of the alloy onto the device pins. Make sure that the alloy has come in contact with every single pin by gently moving the soldering iron around the edges of the device. Avoid touching nearby components on the PCB with the soldering iron.

Apply heat and alloy to the leads.

Chip with alloy applied.

DESOLDERING TIPS: For standard through-hole components, first grasp the component with a pair of needle-nose pliers. Heat the pad beneath the lead you intend to extract and pull gently. The lead should come out. Repeat for the other lead. If solder fills in behind the lead as you extract it, use a spring-loaded solder sucker to remove the excess solder.

For through-hole ICs or multi-pin parts, use a solder sucker or desoldering braid to remove excess from the hole before attempting to extract the part. You can use a small, flat-tip screwdriver or IC extraction tool to help loosen the device from the holes. Be careful to not overheat components, since they can become damaged and may fail during operation.

3. Now that the alloy has been properly applied to all pins of the device, it's time to remove the device from the board. After making sure that the alloy is still molten by reheating all of it with the soldering iron, gently slide the component off the board. You can use a small, jeweler's flat-tip screwdriver to help with the task. If the device is stuck, reheat the alloy and wiggle the part back and forth to help the alloy flow underneath the pads of the device and loosen the connections.

Remove the device from the board.

4. The final step in the desoldering process is to clean the circuit board. This step is important because it will remove any impurities left behind from the Chip Quik process and leave you ready for the next step in your hardware hack.

First, use the soldering iron to remove any stray alloy left on the device pads or anywhere else on the circuit board. Next, apply a thin, even layer of flux to all of the pads that the device was just soldered to. Use the included alcohol swab or a flux-remover spray to remove the flux and clean the area.

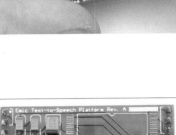

Use flux and an alcohol swab to clean the area.

5. The desoldering process is now complete. The surface-mount device has been removed and the circuit board cleaned. If you intend to reuse the device you just removed, use the soldering iron to remove any stray alloy or solder left over on and in between the pins and ensure there are no solder bridges between pins. If you do not want to reuse the device, simply throw it away.

Circuit board with part successfully removed.

FINISH ☒

Joe Grand (joe@grandideastudio.com) is the president of Grand Idea Studio, Inc., a product-development and intellectual-property licensing firm. He specializes in embedded system design, computer security research, and inventing new concepts and technologies.

Reprinted with permission from *Hardware Hacking*, copyright 2004, Syngress Publishing, ISBN: 1-932266-83-6, pp. 34-40.

MakeShift

By William Lidwell

The Scenario: After a relaxing night of camping in the deep woods, you return to your car to find that it will not start. The battery is dead. "Someone" left the parking lights on overnight. You are 50 miles from the nearest road and have limited food and water. You try to call for help, but your cellphone is out of power and out of range. Snowy weather is scheduled to set in by late evening. The situation is serious.

The Challenge: Create a makeshift solution to recharge the battery and start the car. Tools and materials at your disposal include the objects on the supply list listed below (as well as the car and its components). You have 10 hours. By the way, the car has an automatic transmission — push-starting won't work.

Supply List:

1 Tent	1 Banana
2 Sleeping bags	1 Large bag of potato chips
Sterno (stove and fuel)	2 Liters of bottled water
First-aid kit (Aspirin, adhesive bandages, hydrogen peroxide)	1 Cellular phone
2 Pencils	2 Road flares
6 Pack of cola	A variety of tools (screwdrivers, wrenches, pliers, Swiss Army knife)
1 Dozen limes	Matches
2 Apples	Jumper cables

Email a detailed description of your MakeShift solution with sketches and/or photos to makeshift@makezine.com by March 31. If duplicate solutions are submitted, the winner will be determined by the quality of the explanation and presentation. The most plausible and most creative solutions will win MAKE T-shirts. Think positive, and include your shirt size and contact information with your description. Good luck!

William Lidwell is a consultant with Stuff Creators Design Studio and co-author of the book *Universal Principles of Design*.

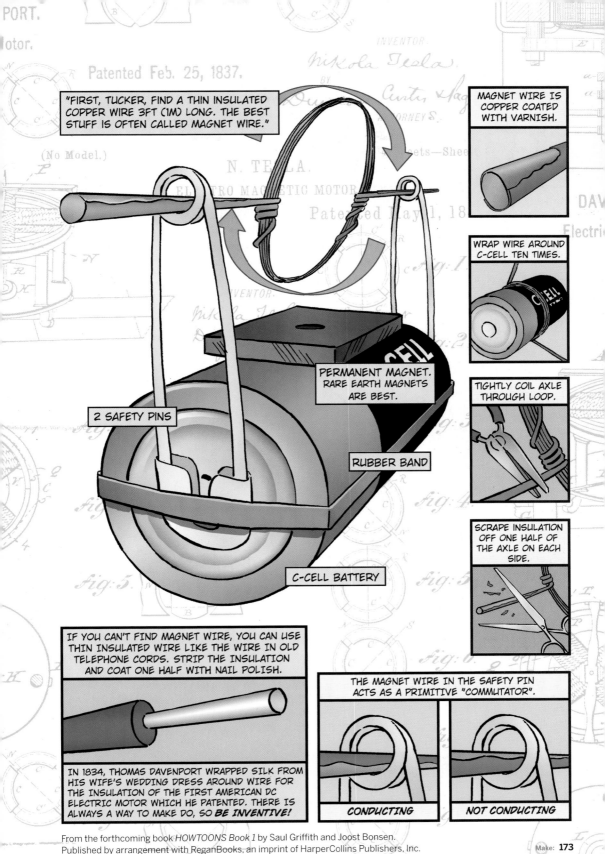

From the forthcoming book *HOWTOONS Book 1* by Saul Griffith and Joost Bonsen.
Published by arrangement with ReganBooks, an imprint of HarperCollins Publishers, Inc.

The best tools, software, gadgets, books, magazines, and websites.

TOOLBOX

An addictively handy computer toolkit.

PC TOOLKIT FOR YOUR POCKET

Victorinox Swiss Army CyberTool
$40, *www.victorinox.com*

I'm on my second CyberTool. (The first was lost, along with my luggage, by Delta.) I absolutely love it. It won't change your life; you probably already have a toolset. The CyberTool's screwdriver is off center and this makes it annoying to turn. A pair of inexpensive needlenose pliers does a better job than the included pliers. And I find the thought of using the toothpick as intended to be utterly disgusting.

So with all these caveats, why have I owned two? Because it is so easy to have around. I leave it out on my desk and reach for it constantly — my fully stocked toolbox in the closet never gets touched. It has a good selection of bits for most applications (although they should have included at least one smaller Torx driver).

In the last month, I've used it to open my PowerBook for a memory upgrade, gain access to a stubborn remote control's battery compartment, slice through an untold number of letters and packages, remove a tiny ingrown hair, and to escape certain death by drowning by using the can opener as a hook to unlock the door to a room that was being filled with water. (Oh wait, never mind, that was a MacGyver re-run.)

—*Michael Rattner*

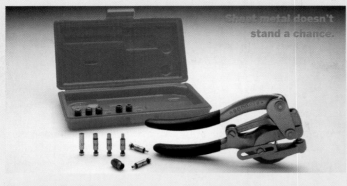
Sheet metal doesn't stand a chance.

Punch Happy

Roper-Whitney #5 Jr. Hole Punch
$48 at *www.roperwhitney.com*
or try *www.mcmaster.com*
(Look under "hand punches")

If you have sheet material you need to make neat holes in, nothing beats a Roper-Whitney #5 Jr. Compact, powerful, reliable, and hand-powered, a #5 Jr. will punch holes through quarters, if that's what you want. (And who doesn't want to do that?)

Designed for working with sheet metal, the #5's role in your projects will expand when you realize just how much it can do. There is no tool that does a cleaner job punching ventilation holes in computer cases. Cladding a ho-hum bit of electronics in material to match your decor is easy when you can make your own mounting holes.

Plastic flowerpots can be hung by cord passed through the smooth holes a #5 will punch in their edges. Washers made from pennies keep bolt heads from tearing through thin material and make good electrical contacts when grounding electronics. Punching heavy cardstock or plastic sheets is trivial for this tool. Wind chimes, made from found objects or flea-market cutlery, are amazingly well-received gifts, as are homemade buttons. It's possible to do intricate punching of sheet stock and wind up with your own absinthe spoon in very little time at all.

Roper-Whitney makes replacement punch sets suitable for punching oblong holes in leather belts, along with many other sizes and shapes. Besides all this, the Roper-Whitney #5 Jr. combines an elegant articulation and the good ergonomics that result from a long presence in the market. Grab one and start ventilating.

—Steve Wood

MAKE SOFTWARE PICK

Mac Across the Living Room

Salling Clicker
$20, *www.salling.com*

If your Mac and mobile device are both Bluetooth-enabled, Salling Clicker will let you control your Mac using your mobile phone or Palm OS PDA. You can use this application to advance your Keynote presentation, browse your iPhoto collection, cruise through your iTunes playlists, and navigate DVD menus. Not only does it give you remote control, you can also view information from these apps right on the phone. You can browse pictures from iPhoto and see album art from iTunes, read RSS headlines, or catch up on your email — all from your mobile device.

What's really impressive about Salling Clicker is the way it takes advantage of your mobile device's features. Does your Palm OS PDA have a color screen? You can preview pictures on the device before showing them on your Mac's display. Does your phone have a jog dial on the side? Use it to adjust the volume in iTunes. Get a phone call while watching a DVD? Clicker will pause the movie while you take the call.

There are controls available for GarageBand, Logic Audio, VLC, and more. One user even created a script that controls the angle of his backyard telescope!

—Justin Ried

Turn your Bluetooth phone into a Macintosh remote.

An easily hackable tool for wood, plastic, metal, and PCB.

From the clever domain name department comes *http://del.icio.us*. Forget Yahoo's categorized links and Google's web directory, *del.icio.us* is a far tastier treat. *del.icio.us* is a collaborative bookmark collection that allows users to file their links under categories of their own creation. This means you can find information here on everything from programming (*del.icio.us/tag/programming*) to Wankel rotary engines (*del.icio.us/tag/wankel_rotary_engine*).

Here's how it works: first, you sign up for a free account. As soon as you're finished, *del.icio.us* will point you to the Post Del.icio.us link that takes you to the bookmark-posting page. Put this bookmarklet somewhere accessible, like in the bookmarks bar of your browser.

Building a web directory one bookmark at a time.

So, let's say you find a site about building hovercrafts. Simply click on the "post del.icio.us" link you got earlier, and type in "hovercraft" as the category. Now that hovercraft link will show up at *del.icio.us/yourusername*. It'll also show up at *del.icio.us/tag/hovercraft*, as well as on the front page of *del.icio.us*.

New links are always coming in, making *del.icio.us* a killer timewaster. Now you can find that link from *any* computer.   —*Alex Handy*

True Grit

**Delta SA150 Shopmaster
1"Belt & 5"Disc Sander**
$89, *www.deltamachinery.com*

Tip: The adhesive-backed disks can get expensive. Buy a can of aerosol stencil glue and cut/coat your own.

I paid CDN$79 for my Delta 5" disk/1" belt sander two years ago, and I use it every day. Yeah, 5" isn't much — I'd be the first to admit to serious disc envy over the Professional 10" model-maker's sanders, and the 1" belt would be absolutely laughable, were it not for one exceptionally cool feature: unlike your regular-type, bench-mount belt sander, which has the belt running horizontally over a steel backplate, this wee beastie has the belt running on a vertical plane with a removable backplate.

It's absolutely brilliant. Imagine having a freestanding, abrasive waterfall with a 4" deep throat. (The throat is how deep into the material you can go before you run into another part of the tool.) As with all tools, developing finesse requires scaling a learning curve — with the backplate removed and a 50-grit belt you can find yourself removing large quantities of material seemingly at random. Caution is the watchword. Once you achieve sander Zen, though, you'll have at your command a freeform shaper-smoother-former of uncommon flexibility. You'll be reaching for the Dremel a lot less frequently when confronted with complex geometry, and it does normal, bench-sander type stuff, too. I've cobbled together jigs for tool sharpening and other, more-specialized tasks.

Caveat: The power switch is prone to intermittency in the presence of dust. Seriously. After the third failure, I dropped a properly sealed Switchcraft toggle into the case and in-lined a footswitch for hands-free activation.
    — *Kaden Harris*

Garmin GPS Goes (More) Proprietary

eTrex Vista C $428,
eTrex Legend C $375,
www.garmin.com

Bad news for travelers: Garmin locks up its GPS data.

Garmin's recent outdoor GPS units sport a USB port instead of the strange proprietary connector they used to have. That sounds great, except that Garmin's gone more proprietary on the protocol they use to send location data over that connection, abandoning NMEA in favor of Garmin's own protocol.

While looking through the Amazon reviews for Garmin's latest Vista C and Legend C, I found some red flags:

"However, the USB connectivity will only connect you to proprietary Garmin cartography software, it is NOT NMEA compatible. (Legend C)"

"It will no longer work with a Macintosh. The software loads and works easily using VPC as did the software for the prior version. However, the USB driver provided by Garmin will not work with a Macintosh and there does not seem to be an alternative, according to the technical support at Garmin. (Vista C)"

Curious, I called Garmin. I didn't get the name of the lucky recipient of my call, which got angrier as it went on, but he confirmed that Garmin has, in fact, dropped NMEA support. He was happy to report that their protocol was indeed proprietary. I asked why they did this, and his reply was that "our engineers decided to support Garmin software." If I wanted that changed,

my only recourse was to request a feature or buy a different unit.

I'll put in the feature request, though I can't say the phone call gave me much hope that Garmin is interested in any such change. We can, of course, use Garmin's protocol documentation, but that also has some interesting bits:

Q: The internet has information about additional protocols and extensions that are not described in the document. Why have these been left out?

A: Part of the goal of the document is to separate what GARMIN thinks is safe versus what is unsafe when interfacing to our GPS products. Any items left out of the document are considered to be "testing aids" for use by our engineering and manufacturing departments only....

6.13 of the Garmin specification does provide the PVT Data Protocol, "an alternative to NMEA so that the user may permanently choose the GARMIN format on the GPS instead of switching back and forth between NMEA format and GARMIN format." That may be the place to focus for people who want to use Garmin units but want to connect them to a broader range of software than Garmin itself provides.

—*Simon St.Laurent*

LED Lantern

**Cabela's 12-LED Lantern
with Remote**
$40, *www.cabelas.com*

Recently, standing on a chair in my bathroom, reaching yet again for an expired light bulb, I thought: there's got to be a better way. And there is — an LED light. The benefits of light-emitting diodes are legion: they burn cold, draw less power than Edisons, and have a lifespan measured in decades. So when I found myself in the market for a reading lamp, I had to have LED.

I came across the perfect solution in the unlikeliest of places: Cabela's, an outdoor supply store that sells the amazing LED Lantern. It features 12 LEDs — three to a side — around a central column for 360° illumination, runs 40 days continuously on four D batteries, and comes with a keychain remote control, all for $39.99. It won't light your apartment, but it's ideal for sticking behind your laptop during those all-night coding sessions, or I guess, actual camping.

—*Geoffrey Litwack*

Tired of changing lightbulbs? Try Cabela's camping lantern.

The after-market add-ons make this flashlight shine.

Blinded by the LED

L4 Digital Lumamax
$160, *www.surefire.com*
Kroll Tailcap Switch:
$4.50, *www.anlighten.com*

Surefire, makers of a complex array of tactical "illumination tools" for the military and police, continue to push the state-of-the-art in ultra-powerful, LED-based flashlights, such as the L4 Digital Lumamax. A scant 3.4 ounces and only slightly bigger than a dry erase marker, the L4 puts a blinding 65 lumens of regulated, pure white light into a smooth, artifact-free beam for up to an hour. The flood beam is ideal for brightly illuminating objects in the 2- to 20-foot range, exactly where my geek lighting tasks usually fall. From hunting lost screws, checking cable runs above a dropped ceiling, or lighting up the back of a server rack, it's tough to beat the broad, brilliant beam of the L4.

Drawbacks? All those photons come to you first-class, in the form of two expensive 123 lithium primary (i.e. non-rechargeable) cells. And, believe it or not, the L4 can be too bright, either for very close work or use around dark-adapted eyes — you do not want to show up at your local astronomy club's star party with one of these. But it's not all bad news. The 123 cells are available via the web from a number of sources (including Surefire) for prices in the range of $1 to $2 each; quite a savings from the $7 my local Safeway wants.

Similarly, an after-market tailcap that significantly enhances the utility of the L4 is available. A two-stage switch provides brightness control. The tailcap also manages to incorporate a tripod socket, lanyard hole, end stand, and switch guard. Mod kits for the stock tailcap are also available for the hardware hacker, as are bare-board resistor carriers if the stock values don't suit you.

Bottom line: This is an ideal light for indoor and close-range outdoor illumination. If you need long-range illumination, consider an incandescent light. Its filament will generally produce a tighter, longer-throw beam for a given reflector size than the rather large emitting area of an LED array.

—*Bob Scott*

Keychain Browser

thumb stealth

Portable Firefox 1.0
Free, *http://johnhaller.com/jh/mozilla/portable_firefox*
Fit Firefox on a USB Drive

Portable Firefox can be installed and run *entirely* from a USB thumb drive on any Windows machine.

You can stroll into your local fern bar/internet cafe/buddy's house, plug in your thumb drive and have *your* browser, your bookmarks, your passwords, etc., all instantly available. Plus, all browser-cache activity is redirected to the thumb drive as well, so all your detritus comes with you when you unplug the drive. You leave no personal "footprints" on the host machine.   —*Bob Scott*

Better Biking Through Science

Bicycling Science: Third Edition, by David Gordon Wilson
$23, ISBN 0262731541,
www.mitpress.com

Released in April 2004, David Gordon Wilson's updated *Bicycling Science* fills the gap between, on the one hand, shop manuals and training guides, and on the other, contemporary literature on human-powered vehicles.

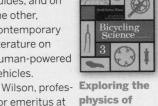

Wilson, professor emeritus at MIT, navigates physics and physiology to produce a hefty source of insight.

Exploring the physics of pedal-powered locomotion.

He splits his book into three sections: the biology of human-power generation including the role of oxygen uptake and distributing, the physics of turning complicated muscle motions into linear velocity, and radical redesigns of the standard diamond-frame bicycle.

Bicycling Science can be used as a handbook for the armchair designer of human-powered vehicles or as a way to answer the nagging science questions that arise after a thoughtful bike ride.

Perhaps its most inspiring use, however, is as a bed-table compendium of standalone investigations into what engineers have come up with on a device that has been perfected, again and again, for decades longer than the internal combustion engine.

—*Simon DeDeo*

Tamperproof screws meet their match.

Screw Buster
Boxer TP62 Security Kit
$30, *www.calcentron.com*

Once I got a Boxer TP62 screw-driver kit, I realized the world was held together with tamperproof screws and started carrying it with me everywhere. Previously, if I came across an obscure tamperproof screw, I would grind an Allen wrench until I could jam it in or mickey mouse some sort of welding rod and Vise-Grip contraption.

The Boxer TP62 is a standard removable bit, plus a ratcheting screwdriver with not only the expected standard Phillips and flat bits, but also 57 high-security tamperproof bits to open damn near every machine meant to remain unopened. From the sinister Snake Eyes Spanner to the three-blade Phillips, there are bits for screws I didn't even realize were removable. With the Boxer, you think, "For now, you bastard screws will remain impervious, steadfastly guarding against the random reordering of tenant listings. But make no mistake, should I desire, I could have every damn one of you removed in seconds. And I would eat you like hot peanuts."   —*Mister Jalopy*

Quirky but cool portable XM radio.

Reliable Routes

Magellan RoadMate 700
$1,299, www.magellangps.com

As I drive, my Magellan RoadMate 700's voice prompt tells me when to turn and also recalculates my route if I happen to stray off course. It has a bright, full-color touchscreen display that gives me several ways to choose a destination. The 10MB hard drive contains street details and points of interest for the entire U.S.

The device comes with a vent mount, or you can buy an optional windshield mount. (I recommend that you opt for the windshield mount because it's easier to use.) Power is supplied via the car's cigarette lighter (which is, alas, the only way to power the device; there is no battery). An optional external antenna is available, but I didn't find it necessary because reception was always good, or even excellent. In fact, this RoadMate model seemed to acquire its satellites more quickly than the NeverLost model I rented with my Hertz.

I recently updated to the latest software by downloading a file from the Magellan site, then running the update while my RoadMate was connected to my PC via a USB cable. The update offered numerous new features, such as improved performance, an integrated 3D display, plus the ability to show and route to POIs on the map. The latter ability is very handy if you are driving around trying to find a place like an ATM, gas station, or restaurant. The RoadMate shows POI icons on the map while you're driving, and lets you display their address/telephone info or reroute to them by finger press.

There are two missing features that would be nice to have. One would be routing using real-time traffic conditions (via a wireless data service). The second would be the integration of a restaurant/lodging guide like Zagat or AAA.

—Joseph Fung

Your friendly connection to the GPS satellites.

XM Everywhere

Delphi XM MyFi
$350, www.xmradio.com/myfi/

I can use the Delphi XM MyFi all through my apartment with no reception problems. The only thing I don't like so far is that it's just a little bit smarter than I like. It's very fussy about what it will and won't do when it's portable, in a home dock, or in a vehicle dock. For example, I get a great signal with the unit just sitting on my desk and using the internal antenna. But, if I put it in the dock to charge it, it immediately generates an "ANTENNA" error message if an external antenna isn't connected to the dock. It still continues to receive just fine; I just can't read the display until I plug it in.

Similarly, it won't do a timer recording unless it's in the home dock. So there will be no automatic recording in the car while I'm at work.

But this is a small gripe ... the thing is really cool overall.

I popped open the home dock and was very interested to find an empty spot for a quad flat pack IC on the circuit board. I wonder what Delphi has up its sleeves? You'll see my Roady2 on eBay shortly. *—Bob Scott*

Explosive Clog Buster

Kleer Drain
$30, www.kleerdrain.com

I went to Home Depot recently to buy $2 worth of hardware (pins for door hinges) and walked out with over $100 worth of stuff, of course. My prime purchase was a Kleer Drain instant drain opener, which combines the fun of explosives with the satisfaction of unclogging a sink.

I was a little wary of spending close to $30 on this gadget, which looks like a cross between a plunger and a pogo stick. I've been burned by neat-looking gizmos in the past, like the garlic bulb de-skinner that looked so promising but ended up doing nothing more than cutting deep grooves into the cloves.

But Home Depot had one of those videos running next to the setup, which showed a lot of clogged sinks giving up their stubborn boluses of greasy hair to the explosive force of a CO_2 cartridge unleashing its entire payload of pressurized gas at once. Watching the guy on the demo using the device, with its rifle-like kickback and puff of condensed carbon dioxide gas, mesmerized me. The next thing I knew, I was racing home with my new Kleer Drain.

I could hardly wait to use it on a slow-draining sink in the bathroom. I duct-taped the overflow drain on the sink, and inserted a CO_2 cartridge into the Kleer Drain. I screwed on the rubber cone and then pressed it into the drain opening.

WHAM! A shower of gray grime flew out of somewhere and splashed against the walls, mirror, and ceiling. I wiped the junk off my face and turned on the faucet. (I should have used the included plastic sheet to cover the sink, but I wanted to see the thing in action). Like a smoking gun, a plume of white carbon dioxide wafted gently up from the bowl. As the mist cleared, I was greeted by the sight of water whooshing down the drain, ending with a nice sucking sound, like the drain was wishing there was more water it could dispose of.

I think I'm in love. Time to stock up on more CO_2 cartridges.

—Mark Frauenfelder

Armed with a handful of CO_2 cartridges and some "Power Disks," you're ready to blast your most stubborn plumbing problems down the drain.

Excellent all around camera, but beware the shutter delay.

The Hardbody
HP 945
$400, www.shopping.hp.com

As two of the more popular "pro-sumer" digital cameras, both the HP 945 and Canon Digital Rebel have the goods. This is not a comparison between the two as much as a look at two offerings at different price points that do a fine job for those who are ready for more megapixels, more features, and more options in their digital photography.

FIRST IMPRESSIONS:
HP 945:

With its unusually shaped body, the 945 is cradled by your hand, but you'll want to keep both hands on the body to achieve good stability for sharper shots. It's a solid-feeling camera and comes nearly fully equipped, only requiring extra batteries and memory cards, like most digital cameras. The LCD is clear and the optical-diopter adjustment in the viewer helps this 5.3-megapixel model produce clean, sharp images.

Canon Digital Rebel:

The Rebel feels more like my old 35mm SLR, only lighter. I found battery life from the provided lithium ion cell to be excellent, and I like the CompactFlash memory card performance. With a whopping 6.3 megapixels and Canon's DirectPrint connection to their photo printers, I was amazed by the quality of the output.

LIKES:
HP 945:

From skylines to eye wrinkles, you can bring the whole scope of a scene together with this larger-diameter lens. The images are crisp and even, with very little ghosting in the highlights, which can appear in some other models. The 2" LCD is adjustable and works great to check, edit, and omit shots as you go. I also like the direct printing to HP Photosmart printers via the available dock. This worked well for me in all applications in OS X including Preview, iPhoto, Photoshop, and GraphicConverter when importing and manipulating my images. Clean,

The Jackrabbit
Canon Digital Rebel
$1,000, www.canonusa.com

sharp, and undistorted images are what you get. Another great feature is the ability to connect the 945 to a television to show off your fine photography.

Canon Digital Rebel:

For its more conventional size

and appearance, the Digital Rebel ends the familiarity right there. The multistage metering and metering options work just as well for the beginner as they do when spot metering like a pro. Where the CDR really excels, though, is in the speed, with sequential flash shots and rapid-fire bursts being no problem at all. The CMOS sensor is outstanding, and the results are nearly dimensional. The variety of options — from lens changes to program/auto and manual modes — offers a lot of camera with great results.

DISLIKES:
HP 945:

The images had excellent clarity; however, the 945 produced results that were +12 percent in cyan under mixed direct light and

Rapid-fire shots and plenty of metering options.

shadows, and slightly (about -4 percent) underexposed in some shots that were in full shade, but had enough light to go without flash. In general, I found most images slightly cool but acceptable in most situations. For macro shots, the auto-focus was quirky but achieved very sharp and clear results once the exposure was corrected. My only real complaint is in the shot-to-shot recovery time. Lag time from focus to shutter has just enough of a delay to be frustrating, but the results make it worthwhile.

Canon Digital Rebel:
While the standard 18-35mm lens does a fine job, it would not be my lens of choice. The full wide-angle does an adequate job, but the lower corners lost clarity in the lower resolution modes. Also, for a $1,000 price point, the CDR doesn't have the solid feel of a camera like you'd expect. This is both good and bad since it is light-weight, but it feels like the plastic you might find on a midlevel con-sumer camera.   —*Daniel M. East*

Candid Digicamera

Sony DSC-V1 Digital Camera
$380, *www.amazon.com*

5 MEGAPIXELS IN A MINI PACKAGE

Planning a vacation in Morocco recently, I knew I'd take loads of photos. When taking candid photos of people in public, dis-cretion is key, and it's hard to remain unobtrusive while han-dling a big, black Nikon N70.

With that in mind, I bought a Sony Cyber-shot DSC-V1 digital camera. At 5 megapixels and 4X optical zoom, it proved perfect for quick shots when sidling through crowded Moroccan souks. Using its movie function, I created a fairly crisp record-ing of a dusk call for prayer as I strolled through Marrakech's exotic Djemma el Fna.

Prints to Dye For

Hi-Touch Imaging 631PL
$110, *www.hi-ti.com*

The HiTi 631: great prints, cheap price.

My friends and relatives still don't think that getting "MIME Encoded DSC10034.JPG" in their email inbox is an appropriate response to "Send me a copy of that picture." With that attitude, I was ready to go back to my mantra from film days: "I'm shooting slides, sorry. Can't make prints, you know."

It's all better now. I took advantage of the plunging prices for dye sublimation printers and purchased a HiTi 631PL printer.

"Dye sub" printers use a roller to press the photo paper against a "ribbon" and a thermal print head. As the paper and ribbon roll through, pixels in the print head are heated, diffusing ("sublimat-ing") the color from the ribbon into a spot on the paper. This process is repeated three times, one pass for each of the primary subtractive colors: cyan, magenta, and yellow.

This process produces a remarkably even, "dotless" continu-ous tone image that is difficult to tell from a traditional pho-tographic print. The HiTi 631 is a relentlessly single-purpose machine. It is designed to do exactly one thing: make extremely high-quality 4x6 photo prints … period. Operation is simple: hit the "print" button in your favorite application, and in less than two minutes, a lab-quality print will drop in the "out" tray.

Pros:
- Compact, quiet, and fast.
- Produces durable, sharp, pixel-less prints with amazing color.
- Cheap (street price well under $200 with controller handset).

Cons:
- Not versatile; produces only 4x6 photos.
- Only connects to Windows computers or works as a standalone.
- Inefficient; one ribbon cassette produces exactly 50 prints, regardless of the amount or type of color in the images.

Bottom line:
If you need to print photos, and don't need anything larger than 4x6, buy it. I can't imagine going back to anything else for photo work.   —*Bob Scott*

Home Library Database

Delicious Library
$40, *www.delicious-monster.com*

Here's how this beautifully de-signed personal library database works: grab a book, scan the URL with your iSight or type the ISBN, and watch the book pop up on a virtual shelf. The software con-nects to *amazon.com* to get the cover and the various metadata. Repeat this for all your books (plus your movies and your video games) and you get a virtual re-presentation of your bookshelves all tagged up. The fun doesn't stop here: you can sort your stuff, create custom shelves (think playlists), and sync up with your iPod. You can even drag friends from your Address Book to create a list of borrowers, then lend out books, and let iCal keep track of the due dates.   —*Peter Orosz*

Lab-O-Rama

**Elenco 300-in-One
Electronic Project Lab**
$75, *www.target.com*

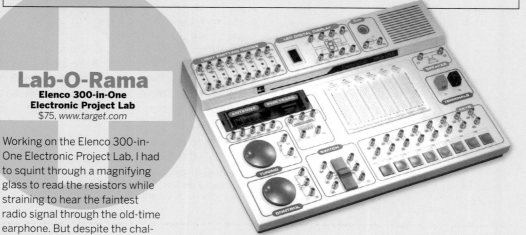

Working on the Elenco 300-in-One Electronic Project Lab, I had to squint through a magnifying glass to read the resistors while straining to hear the faintest radio signal through the old-time earphone. But despite the chal-lenges of getting older, blinder, and deafer, building ridiculous electronics projects is just as fun as when I was a 10-year-old, self-professed inventor.

With a solderless breadboard and handfuls of resistors, capaci-tors, ICs, transistors, and zillions of connecting wires, you can build all sorts of preposterous projects.

Building the ESP Tester (Project #98) or Electronic Cat (Project #82) is quick since the support-ing cast of built-in components — a slide switch, power trans-former, 1.5- to 9-volt power taps, photo cell, etc. — is looped in as needed. After assembling the Funny Transistor Radio (Project #65), the same youthful wonder remains as you tune to one of the two measly stations on your primitive radio.   —*Mister Jalopy*

Have you used something worth keeping in your tool-box? Let us know about it at toolbox@makezine.com.

Simon DeDeo is a graduate student in New Jersey.

Daniel East is a writer for several Mac publications and the founder of the Mid-Atlantic Apple & Macintosh User Groups Team.

Joseph Fung is the managing direc-tor of software product development for Burgiss Group.

Alex Handy is a writer by nature and a geek by trade. He blogs at *www.gism.net*.

Kaden Harris builds unconventional things at *www.eccentricgenius.ca*.

Mister Jalopy breaks the unbroken, repairs the irreparable and explores the mechanical world at *Hooptyrides.com*.

Simon St.Laurent is a web develop-er, network administrator, computer book author, and XML troublemaker living in Ithaca, NY.

Geoffrey Litwack lives at *litwack.org*.

Peter Orosz (peter.orosz@gmail.com) is a writer, doctor, and techno-utopi-an living in Budapest, Hungary, where he can't buy Pop-Tarts.

Michael Rattner is a full-time intel-lectual living in San Francisco.

Justin Ried is editor-in-chief of *TheFeature.com*.

Bob Scott is a statistical construct of various consumer-electronics marketing departments.

Because this is our first issue, we don't have any feedback from readers yet. However, lots of people have written us in anticipation of the debut issue. Here's our favorite: a story from Jeffrey Haemer, a MAKE newsletter subscriber.

Thinking about MAKE brings warm memories of an old friend, BA, the initials not being for anonymity but because that's what he goes by.

BA cut the legs off his sofa so he wouldn't have to sweep under it. It's where he spent a lot of his time.

One day, I was over at his house, visiting, when a loud buzzer went off.

"What's that?"

"Aw, that's my cat-burglar alarm."

BA had put a cat door in an eye-level window for his cat, with a ramp up to it on the outside of the house. It entered into the utility room, so she could jump down onto the washer, and from there to the floor. Going out was easy, too. No reason a cat needs a ground-level entrance, and it keeps out small dogs.

The part about keeping out dogs worked, but he'd begun seeing strange cats in his house. They'd discover the door and come in to eat his cat's food and escape the cold Colorado winter.

After thinking about the problem, he jury-rigged a step-plate just inside the cat door, then hooked it to a big capacitor and a buzzer.

His own cat would come right through the door. She lived there. Strange cats, however, would come halfway through and stand there looking around to see if the coast was clear. This meant they'd stand on the touch plate for long enough to discharge the capacitor and set off the buzzer.

The alarm was still sounding, so BA reached down next to the couch, picked up a plastic squirt gun, then leaned back over the arm of the couch, looked down the hall into the utility room, took aim, and shot the intruder, who quickly pulled back out the door and ran off.

I guess I'd better go hunt up his address and give him a gift subscription for Christmas, eh?

Talk to us about the first issue, story and project ideas, or other things you think the readers of MAKE should know about, at *makezine.com/talk*.

continued from page 37

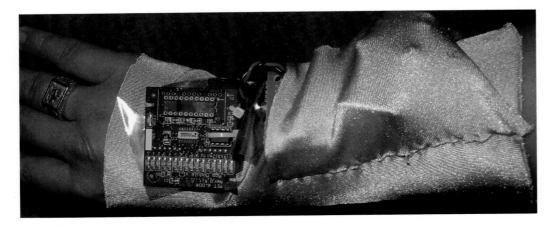

Figure 4: Close-up of the initial kinetic glowstick prototype.

a frequency divider. Thus, choosing bit 16 to be the least significant bit of the frame count meant that a different sprite pattern would be rendered on the LEDs approximately once every eight seconds, or about four bars of music at a typical, trance-techno rhythm of 130 beats per minute.

The greater design challenge was how to attach the hack board and its power supply to something that could withstand the abuse of being swung around on an enthusiastic dancer's hands. The main circuit board was never intended for use on its own, and worse yet, the power supply circuit was implemented using free-hanging wires on the back of a breadboard.

My partner, Nikki Justis, invented a clever little hand-mount using stretchy spandex cloth and some zip ties. It slips on like a fingerless glove, and the circuit boards are sewn in place. The configuration ROM for the FPGA is also secured into its socket with a zip tie to prevent losing precious components in case of an accident on the dance floor. A pair of twisted wires across the back of the wrist carries regulated +5 volt power from an assembly that consists of a 7805 linear voltage regulator, a toggle switch, and a 9-volt cell.

The 9-volt cell is held in place using a zip tie, and the whole regulator assembly is hidden using a folding fabric pouch. This particular arrangement of devices protected the most fragile components (the bread boarded power-supply circuit) as well as moved the mass of the 9-volt battery off of the hand itself and onto the wrist, making a much more comfortable setup for dancing.

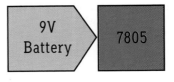

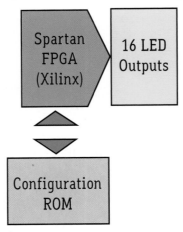

Figure 5: Block diagram of the first prototype's hardware.

When I got this idea back in late 2002, I had bought tickets to see Paul Van Dyke (one of my favorite DJs) play in LA for a huge New Year's party, and I wanted to see if the kinetic glowstick idea actually worked in a party context. I threw together a prototype the day before the party, and Nikki sewed, crimped, and zipped the whole thing together on our drive from San Diego to Los Angeles the night of the party.

rmed with our prototype, we hit the dance floors in Los Angeles and were pretty happy with the results. The prototype had some problems, however. The 9-volt battery was just too massive for long-term comfort. The inefficient 7805 linear regulator gave the whole setup only about three hours of effective battery life.

The spandex gloves, while really cool to a geek like me, were hard for most club-faring folk to swallow. The Spartan FPGA used in the design, and its serial configuration memory, were quite expensive parts for a toy like this. I had to design something with cheaper, lighter parts and with a longer battery life.

The Pager-Case Prototype

In this revision, I wanted not only to have just one color of LED, but three. I wanted to support a full RGB LED implementation with some amount of duty-cycle dithering so we could display a variety of shades of colors. And, just in case the full tri-color setup didn't look as good as I might hope, I wanted to have the option of choosing either full color or a single color at the time of assembly. Thus, I could either populate it with 16 single-color LEDs, or else I could populate it with 8 tri-color LEDs.

I also wanted a fully self-contained package that could be clipped onto a piece of clothing or carried about easily. Unfortunately, tooling up a custom plastic package is a very expensive proposition. So a friend of mine, Mike Wu, helped me acquire a set of

Figure 6: Picture of a completed single-color second prototype.

replacement pager cases from a local pager vendor at almost no cost. The pager cases were perfect: they had a clear plastic window, they had button-holes, and they also came with an optional belt clip that the pager could slip in and out of.

Interestingly, using a pager case to house a circuit like this makes everyone assume that I had hacked a stock pager and rewrote its software to create flash LEDs effects. Of course, it doesn't occur to them that pagers don't have LEDs like this in them or that the circuit board looks a little bit funny. It's often not worth bothering to explain that the circuitry on the inside was not functional as a pager — I just want them to enjoy the show.

The PIC Microcontroller

Also, for the pager-case prototype I needed a new core-sequencer element that combined both the processing power and the storage to drive the LED array into a single package. Remember that in the first prototype, this was handled by a combination of an FPGA and a configuration ROM.

Figure 7: Block diagram of the second-generation prototype. The PIC 16F876A takes the place of the 24-bit counter and sprite ROM, and the 74HC595s are employed as a cost-saving measure to reduce the pin count required for the PIC device.

After searching through a number of low-cost, Flash-based microcontrollers and FPGA options, I settled on the PIC 16F876A part by Microchip. This device is part of Microchip's famous PIC family of devices, a series of very lightweight programmable microcontrollers that integrate a lot of features for a low price.

For those not familiar with microcontrollers, you can think of this as basically a little computer in a single chip. This particular device features 14.3Kb of program memory, 368 bytes of SRAM, and a 256-byte EEPROM — plenty of storage space for this application. It is also available in a cheap 28-pin TSOP (Thin, Small-Outline Package), and it can operate over a wide voltage range (the importance of this will be explained in a minute).

Surprisingly, it turned out to be cheaper in the end to populate banks of 8-bit shift registers (part number 74HC595) to drive all the LEDs than to buy a PIC with sufficient I/O pins to drive up to 24 individual LEDs (three colors by eight elements is 24 total driving lines).

It is counterintuitive that quadrupling the number of parts on the board would lead to a cheaper solution, but the problem with getting parts with a higher I/O count is two-fold: first, devices with higher I/O counts tended to include more features that were not useful for this design, and those useless features cost us money.

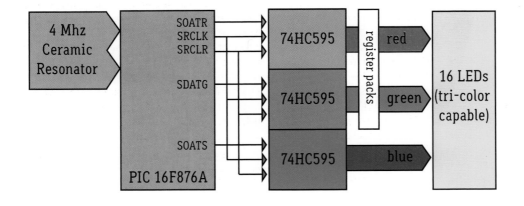

Second, these PICs are so cheap that the cost of the package was a good part of the overall part cost, and package price has a rough correlation with pin count. Also, the 74HC595 parts are part of the venerable "74xx" logic family tree, and these days they are essentially commodity parts with a very economical price. The resulting block diagram of the system is shown in Figure 7.

Enough Power to Party All Night Long

Power management was the biggest design headache for this prototype. Since we decided to use the pager-case design, our battery type was already chosen: one AAA alkaline cell. The Kinetic Glowsticks needed to last at least one long night of partying, so I had set the battery life expectation for this device at 5 hours minimum. Considering that the first prototype only lasted 3 hours with a battery that had 4 to 6 times the power-delivery capacity, I had to use a few tricks to reach this goal.

The first hack was the most obvious: use an efficient switching regulator. I decided upon using a MAX1676EUB high-efficiency compact step-up DC-DC converter made by Maxim Integrated Circuits. This device can take a voltage as low as 0.7 volts and convert it into any higher voltage from 2 to 5.5 volts.

I had to be careful about the parts selection for this regulator because in the tri-color LED configuration, I could encounter rather high peak currents when all 24 LEDs were being driven at maximum brightness. At the same time, this whole thing had to fit inside a pager case. The most challenging part was choosing the right inductor for the job; I eventually settled upon a Sumida CDRH74 series inductor.

Even though the conversion efficiency of the system was improved from about 50 percent to better than 90 percent, I was still not getting the battery life I wanted. The second power-saving hack is a little bit tricky: I run the PIC and the shift registers at the exact forward voltage required by the LEDs. Typically, system designers run digital circuitry at some "standard" voltage, such as 3.3 volts. This is actually quite inefficient for driving LEDs since different color LEDs consume a different amount of power.

The color of an LED is correlated to the "bandgap voltage" of the particular semiconductor alloy used to build the LED. The longer the emitted light's wavelength, the lower the bandgap voltage and the lower the required forward voltage. Thus, every color of LED has a particular forward-operating voltage. In general, red LEDs, with the longest wavelength at around 650nm, can run at about 1.7 volts; green at about 2.2 volts; and blue, with the shortest wavelength at about 470nm, requires upwards of 3.5 volts.

Clearly, running the PIC at a traditional 3.3 volts would be wasteful if only a bank of red LEDs was being driven; roughly 45 percent (1.6 out of 3.3 volts) of the system power would be wasted in the series resistors used to limit the current to the LEDs!

In order to optimize this situation, the MAX1676 was used in its adjustable voltage mode, and the system power was optimized for the type of LED used. In other words, if only red LEDs were being driven, the system voltage is set to 1.7 volts so that no power is wasted in matching the system's drive voltage to the LED's forward-operating voltage.

The other advantage of optimizing the system power for the LED forward-drive voltage is the elimination of current-limiting resistors on the highest voltage LED, which saves a little bit in system cost and board area.

Case Closed

A few other features were added in this revision: an in-circuit programming header so the displayed patterns could be tweaked, and buttons so that users could choose the patterns to cycle through.

The entire circuit was designed and implemented over a weekend, and it all fits in a 1.2"x1.8" two-layer circuit board footprint, including the battery holder. The resulting design is shown in Figure 6.

The system worked fairly well. The tighter LED pattern for this revision of the board gives the resulting image a cleaner appearance. Better yet, the system beat my battery-life expectations: one of my friends had accidentally left the device on overnight, and the next morning you could still see the patterns dimly glowing.

A Bill of Materials and Code Listings for Bunnie's Workbench can be found at the MAKE website, makezine.com/01/bunnie.

Andrew "Bunnie" Huang is best known for his hacks that revealed basic Microsoft Xbox security flaws. He graduated from MIT in 2002 with a PhD in Computer Architecture.

MAKER CHALLENGE

Solving problems, fulfilling wishes.

Do you find yourself wishing for some kind of machine or system to solve a problem or fulfill a wish?

If you have a problem, tell us about it. And if you have a good solution to one of the challenges submitted below, tell us about that too. We'll run our favorite problems and solutions in the next issue and on our website. Send your stuff to challenge@makezine.com.

A Stable Bike » I wonder if there is a way to stabilize a bike so that it can stay upright without extra wheels. The application I have in mind is for disabled kids who don't have the balance skills and muscle control it takes to balance a bike. This would enable them to ride with their friends without the social stigma of riding a three-wheeler or having training wheels. Maybe gyroscopes or a rotating motor?
— *Philippe Habib*

Super 8 Film to DVD » I'd love it if someone could develop a really high-quality way to transfer old movies (8mm and 16mm) to digital at home.
— *Gary A. Peare*

Inexpensive Way to Track Pets » I adopted an abused dog that ran away repeatedly. Searching for her was a lengthy and heart-rending process, which ultimately ended in her death on a road. It was so frustrating that with all the technology available, the only ways I had to find her were posting signs and calling shelters. It took weeks to get sightings that were often several days old.

I've heard of Wi-Fi-type networks to track pets, but that just isn't going to happen soon enough for me, if it even makes it this far into the sticks of rural Michigan.
— *Anne Norman*

Pinhole Digital Camera » I have had discussions recently with a number of other camphone enthusiasts who all love them for the poor quality — the artifacts in the images, the unexpected results. The problem is, the images are just too small. An idea came out of these discussions of what would be really cool: a repurposed digicam that has a larger chip modified to work as a pinhole camera by removing the lens. Is such a thing possible? I don't know. I don't have the skills and neither do any of the guys I know who are interested in this since most of us are software guys. Seems like a good project for MAKE magazine.
— *Marc Goodner*

Antigravity Lifter » Here's a challenge: create the strongest "lifter" — a simple-to-build antigravity machine based on the Beifield-Brown effect.

How to build: *jnaudin.free. fr/html/lftbld.htm*. Check out many videos at the American Antigravity website. There is a growing community around lifters because they're so cool and easy to build. Plus there are many variations on the design work, so the trick is finding which ones work best.
— *Derek Martin*

Toys are big business on eBay, raking in nearly $1.4 billion annual sales worldwide.* The Toys & Hobbies category is the ninth largest on eBay. In the fourth quarter of 2004, radio-controlled toys was the third largest subcategory in the Toys & Hobbies category in the U.S.

PERCENTAGE GROWTH RATE BY WEEK

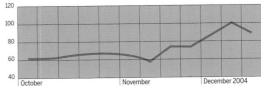

October — November — December 2004

This graph shows the percentage growth rate in successful listings week-over-week for RC Toys in the fourth quarter (scale shows highest week equals 100.) Note the obvious build-up toward Christmas. 72% of the listings are auctions; 58% of them succeed. 15% of the items are listed at a fixed price and 40% succeed. RC aircraft accounts for nearly a third of the sales with four airplanes listed for every helicopter. 66% of helicopter listings succeed compared to 60% for airplanes.

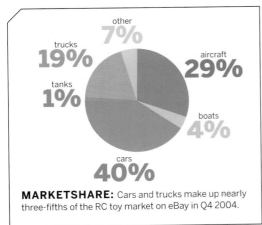

other **7%**
trucks **19%**
aircraft **29%**
tanks **1%**
boats **4%**
cars **40%**

MARKETSHARE: Cars and trucks make up nearly three-fifths of the RC toy market on eBay in Q4 2004.

TAKING OFF: The Raptor 30 V2 Gas/Nitro is the most popular RC helicopter. Made by Thunder Tiger, it is approximately 4 feet long and can cost as much as $3,500 fully equipped.

The most expensive item in the RC Toys subcategory was a $14,000 helicopter that was specially equipped for aerial photography. It did not sell.

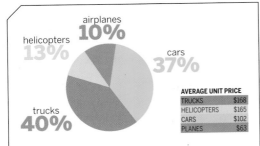

airplanes **10%**
helicopters **13%**
cars **37%**
trucks **40%**

AVERAGE UNIT PRICE

TRUCKS	$168
HELICOPTERS	$165
CARS	$102
PLANES	$63

SALES FOR ASSEMBLED UNITS Listings include parts and supplies as well as kits and completely assembled units. Separating listings for "assembled" units provides a more accurate reading of prices. This chart shows the percentage of sales for assembled units by type. Helicopter listings were up in December to 2,287 from and average of 945 for the two months previous. On average, 3,744 airplanes were listed each month in Q4.

PROFILE: RAPTOR 30

RAPTOR 30	OCTOBER	NOVEMBER	DECEMBER
AVG PRICE	$447	$513	$529
LOW/HIGH PRICE	$150/$1,275	$178/$1,325	$150/$1,500
TOTAL LISTINGS	91	114	121
SUCCESS RATE	76%	64%	72%

This table shows the price and availability of Raptor 30 units and accessories over a three-month period. Note that required components such as transmitters and gyros may not be included with the item. One seller who spent $1,500 on his Raptor 30 and its equipment said, "I don't have the time to fly, so my loss is your HUGE gain!"

Source: Marketplace research by terapeak.com.
Thank you to Chris Smith of Terapeak for assistance.
*eBay Q4 Financial Report

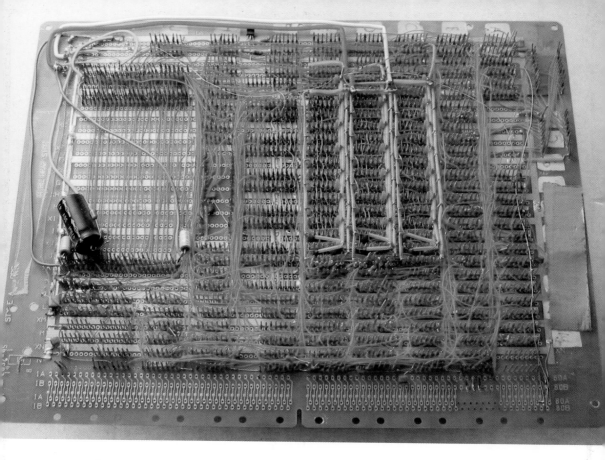

In 1979 I was an 11-year-old who desperately wanted an Apple II. My parents wanted to buy me one, but $2,000 was just too much money. Then one day my dad came home with a pile of photocopies of the poster-sized wiring diagram that shipped with every Apple II. He taped it together, began dropping wire-wrap sockets into a big prototyping PCB, and we were building one ourselves.

I helped a bit, but my dad did most of the work. He sat at the kitchen table late into the night for months, wire wrapping the board and tracing the diagram in yellow pencil crayon as he finished each line. The wire-wrap gun looked like a ray gun. I'd hear it steadily zip as I was falling asleep. When the diagram was solid yellow, we started checking continuity. I remember buzzing out the board with a multimeter as Dad called out endless wire start- and end-coordinates from the diagram and then marked them in orange if they worked.

HOMEBREW

My First Computer
By Gareth Palidwor

When it was finally finished, it was an ugly piece of hardware with a giant, old teletype keyboard, a case-less CRT he pulled out of a dumpster somewhere, and a blue Fisher-Price kiddy tape recorder for "storage." The power supply was a separate box connected by a long wire.

It worked for a couple of years before corrosion in the wire-wrap connections started hanging it too often. By then the guys at my dad's workplace had used in-house CAD software to replicate the Apple II board and had a couple hundred made. There was hell to pay when management found out. We cannibalized most of the chips for the new board and bought a proper case, but I couldn't bring myself to throw out the old board. I still have it. It's kinda busted up from a dozen moves and covered with dust and cobwebs. But it's my first computer.

Do you have your own Homebrew story to share? Send it to us at homebrew@makezine.com.

Photograph by Gareth Palidwor